LEAN ROADMAP

THE LEAN LEADERS GUIDEBOOK

ELEVEN BUILDING BLOCKS FOR A SUCCESSFUL LEAN ROADMAP DESIGN

LEAN ROADMAP

THE LEAN LEADERS GUIDEBOOK

ELEVEN BUILDING BLOCKS FOR A SUCCESSFUL LEAN ROADMAP DESIGN

HOWARD M. THOMES

Lean Roadmap
Published through Lulu.com

Book Design and Layout by
www.integrativeink.com

ISBN 1-4116-2253-7

TABLE OF CONTENTS

TABLE OF FIGURES

DEDICATION

This book is dedicated to my loving wife Carolyn.

ABOUT LEAN ROADMAP

Part I Lean Roadmap Building Blocks Overview
Part I offers an overview of the building block processes required for a complete lean design for your business, relates business improvements to Lean Roadmap building blocks, and is a non-technical "nuts and bolts" overview of the importance and simplicity of these building blocks in improving your business.

Part II Lean Roadmap Management
Part II describes how lean organizational assignments are linked to Lean Roadmap building blocks and covers how leadership and employees function as part of the Lean Roadmap design and implementation.

Part III Lean Roadmap Value Stream Mapping (VSM)
Part III describes the VSM process used for "out of the box" thinking, resulting in an internal team delivering a future-state vision for material and information flow that significantly reduces lead time and costs. This future-state vision is the basis for the detailed design required and defined in Parts IV and V.

Part IV Lean Roadmap Supply Chain Management
Material Flow **Design Process Steps**
Part IV covers material flow related to cell design, plant layout, kanban, and cell management from suppliers to and through the manufacturing process and to the customer, utilizing cellular manufacturing, kanban replenishment, and ATC scheduling to final assembly cell capacity. How to match capacity to demand and deliver on time to the customer.

Part V Lean Roadmap Supply Chain Management *Information Flow* **Design Process Steps**

Part V covers configuring MRP/ERP for lean. Information flow is vital to supply chain design, planning, and management. **Revolutionary concepts that simplify the process are described in this section.**

INTRODUCTION TO LEAN ROADMAP

The primary objective of a Lean Roadmap is to achieve the shortest production lead-time in your addressed market space and to deliver on time to the customer's request date with little or even no finished goods inventory. Additional objectives of a successful Lean Roadmap implementation are reduced overhead structure, reduced quality costs, productivity improvements, and reduced floor space required to operate your business.

Part I of **Lean Roadmap** is an overview of the eleven essential building blocks required for a successful Lean Roadmap design. A successful design and implementation will yield significant improvements in your business. Use the first part of the book to achieve an understanding of how the building blocks complement one another and provide a straightforward roadmap for lean design.

Lean design and implementation in your business is not difficult to accomplish. The 11 Lean Roadmap building blocks are clearly detailed in this book. These building blocks are the required elements for the design, planning, and daily management of a successful supply-chain management system.

Lean Roadmap Business Improvement Deliverables

▪ Eliminate or significantly reduce both work in process and finished goods inventory.
▪ Reduce lead times from weeks to days/hours.
▪ Significantly improve customer on-time delivery (to the customer's date).

- Eliminate wasteful steps in the manufacturing process and realize gains in productivity.
- Reduce floor space required, making room for additional product lines with the same bricks and mortar.
- Configure MRP/ERP for lean. Utilize your current business software investment and realize significant reductions in excess overhead. Use the power of your current business software to establish a required supply chain configuration.
- Convert from a forecast for finished goods inventory to a forecast for kanban and assemble or make-to-order business.
- Seamless and accurate scheduling of customer orders at order entry, matching capacity to demand, using the Assemble to Capacity process (ATC).
- Assemble on-demand product configurations the customer orders.
- Point-of-use inventory at the production cells controlled at the point of assembly, and managed/reordered by the people who assemble/manufacture the product.
- Inventory replacement via kanban; only material consumed by the customer is reordered.
- Measurement, control, and improvement of performance measurements linked from plant to cell level.

Lean Roadmap will clearly detail the business process building-block designs required for your company to achieve significant improvements. The following table is an example of improvement types and magnitude of improvements you should expect, depending on the current state of your business. The listed improvements are easy to achieve utilizing the Lean Roadmap building blocks for design, planning, and management of your supply chain. The chart values are based on historical achievements experienced in working with actual businesses.

Performance Measurement Widgets	Pre- Lean Roadmap Current State Value
Quality Costs, Scrap, Warranty-Annual	$176,000
On Time Delivery to Customers	53%
Direct Labor Employees	42
Indirect Labor Support	8
Salaried Support	1
*Inventory Finished Goods $	$3,475,346
* Inventory WIP $	$476,000
* Inventory Raw $	$1,500,456
Weighted Avg. Lead-Time Days Manuf.	27
Weighted Avg. Lead-Time Days Suppliers	58
Distance Traveled to Make a Product	6500'
Floor Space Value Added for Production	29500 sq ft
Floor Space Non-Value Added	45000 sq ft
Number of Operations to Schedule	12

Lean Roadmap will explain how to:

■ Define and calculate performance measurements that link to required business improvements.

■ Enable a lean organizational structure that places ownership for plant and business improvement where it belongs, yielding consistent Lean Roadmap design and shortened implementation times.

■ Utilize a disciplined process to quantify current process steps, costs, and lead-times used to manufacture products, develop a future state vision (floor plan), project expected savings, cost-to-implement, and timeline for implementation. Thus, you know the potential $

improvement and cost to implement before starting the process.

■ Design a lean supply chain planning and management process for products that yields significant improvements in inventory turns, productivity, and on-time customer delivery.

■ Configure and supplement your current MRP/ERP business software for lean.

■ Plan a simple and effective lean supply chain that matches customer demand to available capacity, replenishing material as the customer purchases products.

■ Manage a lean supply chain: accurate customer scheduling at order entry, building to customer demand, and replacing material as it is consumed.

Lean Roadmap is designed to be an easy *study*, and I suggest you keep a notebook and calculator close by as you read. The Lean Roadmap processes and calculations described are easy to follow; your notebook will record ideas that apply to your business.

Whether you are a business leader or a lean leader, your understanding of the Lean Roadmap building block steps and logical design calculations will arm you with the knowledge to steer a successful lean design for your business. The hours you commit to the understanding of the Lean Roadmap building blocks will pay enormous dividends in the future.

Lean Roadmap is a proven and logical building block process, complete with respect to both material flow (supplier to customer) and information flow (customer to supplier), defined step by step. When you understand the Lean Roadmap supply chain process and develop a design for your business, all that remains is to do it.

The difficulties encountered with a lean implementation generally occur with the information flow processes of *forecasting, customer order entry, scheduling, and materials management*. **Lean Roadmap** explains in detail the information flow business processes required.

In the past, no matter how well we planned and managed material flow through the supply chain, information flow process adversely affected us in several ways:

1. We booked customer orders to infinite capacity.
2. We experienced material shortages and inadequate replenishment of materials required to meet customer demand.
3. We used supplier lead-times of weeks. Self-imposed lead-times of weeks, designed to assist in on-time delivery, actually have the opposite effect. Instead of lead-times of weeks, only hours or days are required to satisfy customer requirements for product.

Without a simplified and effective information flow process that supports the material flow in both planning and execution, the supply chain management process will continue to experience failure. **Lean Roadmap** solves these problems.

If you are wondering why **Lean Roadmap** is not a thicker book, it's because the process is quite simple to understand. The essence of lean is waste reduction and simplicity. Lean supply-chain management is not complicated, and when you read and understand this book's contents and the logic of the process steps, I hope you will agree that more pages would simply be wasteful—and we live lean.

I suggest you make a copy of the glossary of terms located in the back of the book for easy reference. It will provide you with definitions used in this book and is the basis for a common Lean Roadmap vocabulary for your business.

Note: A serious management team dedicated to a Lean Roadmap outcome should plan around a 1-year timeframe for significant implementation and realization of benefits as defined by your performance measurements and detailed in a future state design. As you implement lean in a value stream, the firefighting is replaced with time for planning and managing the business.

Let's get started. Part I of **Lean Roadmap** is an overview of the Lean Roadmap supply chain processes as applied to a typical manufacturing business.

PART I
THE ELEVEN BUILDING BLOCKS OF LEAN ROADMAP FOR SUPPLY CHAIN DESIGN, PLANNING, AND MANAGEMENT

The following lists the eleven essential building blocks for a successful Lean Design. All of these building blocks interact with one another, complement one another, and lead to a truly Just-in-Time Supply Chain.

1. Lean Roadmap Organization Structure
2. Business Performance Measurements

Value Stream Mapping (VSM)

3. Product Planning Families
4. Product Planning Family Sales Forecast
5. Floor Plan and Cells Defined PPQ: Product Process Quantity

Material Flow VSM

6. Cellular Layout; Floor Plan Design

Information Flow VSM

7. Sales & Operations Planning/Kanban Calculations
8. Available to Capacity (ATC) Customer Order Scheduling
9. Customer Order Consolidation Grid

10. Kanban Process
11. Continuous Improvement Management System

The **Lean Roadmap** building blocks are illustrated in the logical order of development.

Lean Roadmap 11 Building Blocks

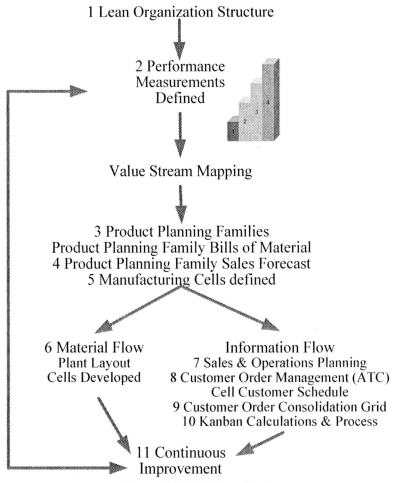

1 Lean Organization Structure

2 Performance Measurements Defined

Value Stream Mapping

3 Product Planning Families
Product Planning Family Bills of Material
4 Product Planning Family Sales Forecast
5 Manufacturing Cells defined

6 Material Flow
Plant Layout
Cells Developed

Information Flow
7 Sales & Operations Planning
8 Customer Order Management (ATC)
Cell Customer Schedule
9 Customer Order Consolidation Grid
10 Kanban Calculations & Process

11 Continuous Improvement

Figure 1: 11 Building Blocks

Bookmark and study the Lean Roadmap glossary of terms found in the back of this book. It is important to establish a common vocabulary for communications within your business.

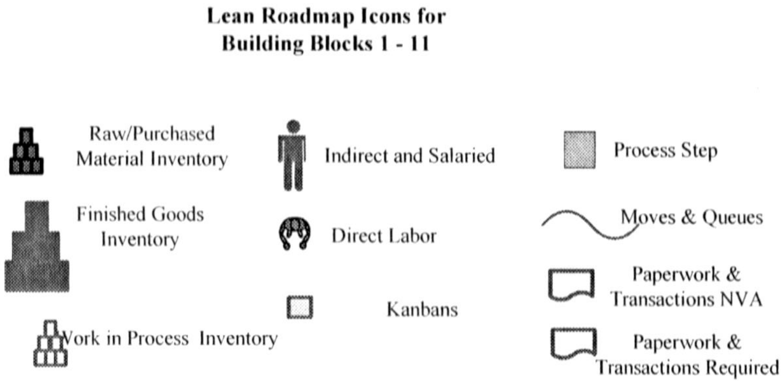

**Lean Roadmap Icons for
Building Blocks 1 - 11**

Raw/Purchased Material Inventory

Indirect and Salaried

Process Step

Finished Goods Inventory

Direct Labor

Moves & Queues

Work in Process Inventory

Kanbans

Paperwork & Transactions NVA

Paperwork & Transactions Required

Figure 2: Lean Roadmap Icons

Lean Roadmap Building Blocks
A Graphic Illustration of Building Blocks 1 - 10

1 Lean Roadmap
Organization Structure

1 Select qualified employees to manage design and implement Lean Roadmap building blocks as defined in Part II of the book.
The result is consistency and shortened implementation time.

2 Lean Roadmap
Business performance Measurements

Determine performance measurements for the businesses that are to be improved as a result of the Lean Roadmap implementation.

Figure 3: Building Blocks 1 and 2

Material Flow & Cell Design: Building Blocks 3 –7

Material flow is the physical coupling of sequential operations as material travels from receiving to shipping. This process eliminates non-value added operations, reduces lead-time, increases productivity, reduces floor space requirements, manages inventory, and reduces/eliminates material stock-outs.

3 Defining and grouping Product Planning Families

1 Products are grouped into Planning Families by build configuration & physical size

2 Product planning families are used to group inventory items and process steps required to produce the families

4 Product Planning Family Forecast Quantity

Product planning family sales forecasts are used to determine the required capacity (cell design), kanban sizes, and organization required to support the sales forecast, and supplier planning

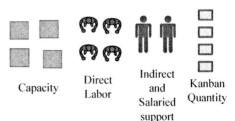

Figure 4: Building Blocks 3–7

5 Family Cell Design

Product family cell concepts are
developed with point of use kanbans

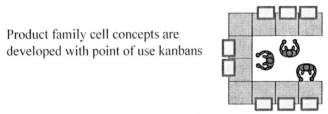

Figure 5: Family Cell Design

Cellular Floor Plan, Plant Material Flow

The factory conceptual floor plan and material flow is defined

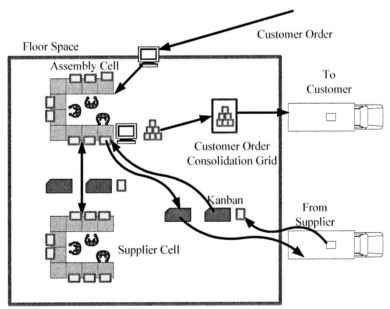

Figure 6: Cellular Floor Plan

Information Flow & Supply Chain Management: Building Blocks 7 - 10

The following illustration is a simple explanation of each building block's role in the Lean Roadmap information flow supply chain management process. This information design for Lean Roadmap manufacturing is the least understood and perhaps the most critical aspect of a successful lean implementation. The information flow process consists of the three basic processes required to plan and manage the material supply chain:

7. Sales & Operations Planning (the supply chain plan);
8. Customer Order Management (ATC, or Available to Capacity Customer Order Entry); and
9. Customer Order Consolidation Grid.
10. Kanban

7 Sales & Operations Planning

1 Sales & Operations Planning used to adjust the capacity and material in the supply chain

2 Manufacturing kanban levels are adjusted to meet the Sales Plan

3 Final Assembly Cell staffing levels are determined and made available

4 The supplier 1 line per item planning report is updated and sent to the supplier who then adjusts their supply chain material and capacity levels.

5 The available to capacity per week for each final assembly cell is updated with a new capacity per week in units.

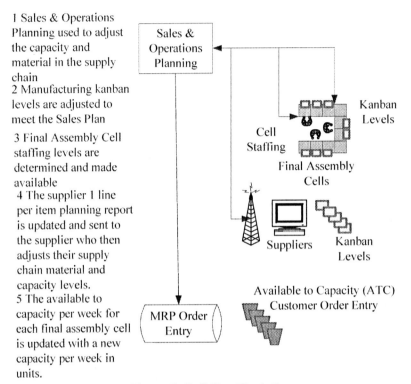

Figure 7: Building Block 7

The important concept to grasp with Available-to-Capacity (ATC) is that the capacity and material kanban levels in each final assembly cell are adjusted at sales and operations planning each month. The available-to-capacity measured in units per week is adjusted at sales and operations planning intervals. In addition, when customer orders exceed capacity for any week, the order entry person is alerted, and the master scheduler works with the operations people to resolve the capacity-required situation. By using ATC the final assembly cells are never overbooked without knowledge of doing so, and appropriate actions can be taken to accommodate the customer.

8 Available to Capacity (ATC)

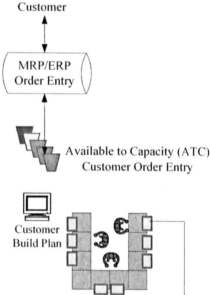

1 Customer orders are accurately scheduled as received, consuming the capacity as determined in S&OP, an accurate order confirmation is returned to the customer

2 Customer orders are accurately scheduled for each final assembly cell

3 Final Assembly cells build product as scheduled based on customer demand and customer request date

9 Customer Order Consolidation Grid

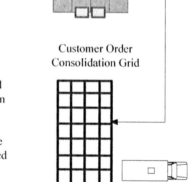

4 Customer orders are assembled and sent to a customer order consolidation grid for shipment to the customer. This avoids the need for storage in racks, and retrieval for shipment. The grid location is automatically assigned at order entry by the ATC logic

Figure 8: Building Blocks 8 and 9

10 Kanban Process

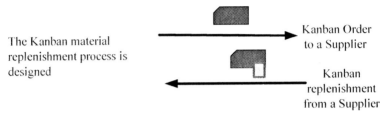

The Kanban material
replenishment process is
designed

Kanban Order
to a Supplier

Kanban
replenishment
from a Supplier

Figure 9: Building Block 10

Continuous Improvement: Building Block 11

One of two continuous processes is at work in every manufacturing business. The first and most insidious is Continuous *Dis-improvement;* this is the daily process of continuing failure of business processes due to the lack of a continuous improvement process. Business processes are continually being fixed, patched, and altered to prevent the one-off occurrence from happening again, adding indirect and salaried resources to cope with the failures that are now built into the process. Over time these broken processes become the norm and are accepted as the cost of doing business.

When any lean implementation is completed in an area or value stream, it will almost immediately begin to revert back to the prior process and deteriorate over time, adding cost and lead-time back into the process.

The only effective way to prevent the decay of business processes from occurring is to implement a closed-loop continuous improvement management system of waste identification and elimination. That process drills from the president down through the organization to include all people and equipment working in the processes, in both material flow and information flow processes. There are many resources available to assist you in design and implementation of this crucial business process, and I urge you to put the structure in place to continually measure results and reduce waste in mainstream business processes.

Applying Lean Roadmap Building Blocks To a Typical Business

Let's study a typical example. The business we are going to convert to a Lean Roadmap design manufactures high-end specialty yard and garden products, for sale through magazines, yard and garden centers, and specialty shops. We'll call it Paradise Products.

The reasons for evaluating the business for a Lean Roadmap transformation are:

1. Customer complaints regarding poor on-time delivery to commitments given
2. Customers complain that lead-times for product out-of-stock are not competitive
3. The sales force is complaining of lost sales due to poor service levels
4. The business suffers from dwindling profit margins and loss of market share
5. Increasing inventory levels
6. Exposure to obsolete finished goods inventory
7. Poor employee morale, and a high level of finger-pointing between sales and operations.

There is, however, one piece of good news. The company president has been replaced with a president focused on business improvement, with an emphasis on business process improvement and supply chain management.

Relative information regarding the business:

1. Manufactures finished goods inventory from a sales forecast.
2. Customer orders are filled from finished goods inventory.
3. When inventory is not available, a production order for product is forced through the factory, or the customer

    waits for the next planned manufacture of products to be made.

4. Customer orders are taken without regard to inventory available or capacity available, assuming an infinite capacity.
5. Customer orders are constantly re-scheduled to meet required dates. This is caused by not matching available inventory and/or capacity to customer orders and date required.
6. The factory process equipment is grouped by functional use—machine shop, injection mold, wind, assembly, and test—and not by process steps required to produce the products.
7. Inventory is stored in raw, work-in-process, and finished goods locations in a dedicated stockroom. As raw materials are converted to sub-assemblies, they are returned to stores and reissued to a final assembly order to replace finished goods.
8. There are no business performance measurements that link from president to all employees in the business.
9. There is no formal business improvement process in place for identification and capture of opportunities.

Lean Roadmap Business Process Evaluation

The new president of Paradise Products has initiated a Lean Roadmap Business Process Evaluation to establish a baseline current-state condition as compared to a fully implemented lean business. This evaluation is a good indicator of what is required to bring the business into a lean state. The evaluation process also establishes a good communication and discovery tool for employees engaged in the fact-finding. **The president has held several all-hands meetings with employees to make clear to them the mission and objectives going forward, and to ask for their assistance and participation in the process.**

    Prior to starting the Lean Roadmap design, the management team utilized the "Lean Roadmap Business Process Evaluation" tool to determine where current business processes varied from the Lean Roadmap 11 building block processes.

The following chart shows the rating the management team derived. To properly utilize the rating tool, a product planning family of electric leaf blowers was process mapped, utilizing a technique called value stream mapping (described in Part III).

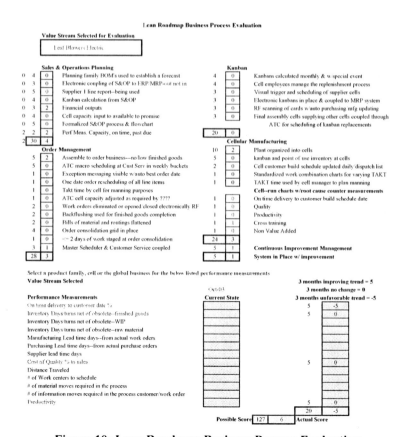

Figure 10: Lean Roadmap Business Process Evaluation

The evaluation yielded 6 points out of a possible score of 127 points. The important understanding here is that a business can be successful without being lean; however, to get to a lean state and improve both the business profits and balance sheet, lean business processes need to be designed and implemented and the appropriate measurements put in place to measure progress.

Lean Roadmap Building Blocks: Future State Design

The president and management team have determined that improvements are required for all measurements listed in the Performance Measurements Chart above. They have determined to utilize Lean Roadmap building blocks for the lean business design.

In addition, they want to implement the Lean Roadmap business practices listed below. They will utilize the building block process steps to determine current and future-state financial impact on the business and how business practices will affect the objectives defined for improvement.

Lean Roadmap Building Block	Performance Measurement Widgets
1, 2, 11	Quality Costs, Scrap, Warranty-Annual
2, 3, 4, 5, 6, 7-9	On Time Delivery to Customers
2, 6, 8-11	Direct Labor Employees
1-11	Indirect Labor Support
1-11	Salaried Support
3, 4, 6, 7, 8,10	*Inventory Finished Goods $
6, 10	* Inventory WIP $
7, 10	* Inventory Raw $
6, 10	Weighted Avg. Lead-Time Days Manuf.
3, 4, 7, 10	Weighted Avg. Lead-Time Days Suppliers
6	Distance Traveled to Make a Product
6	Floor Space Value Added for Production
6, 9, 10	Floor Space Non-Value Added
6	Number of Operations to Schedule

Lean Roadmap Building Block	Business Process Improvements
2-8, 10	Make to customer order, no finished goods
6-8	Customer order scheduling at order entry, matching demand to capacity
4, 6, 7, 8, 10	On time delivery to the customer
3, 4, 7	Supplier planning coupled to business planning
3, 4, 5, 6, 10	linked to final assembly via kanban, lead-time must be reduced, and material shortages are reduced,
10	Kanban used to re-order material
6 thru 10	Reduction in supply chain lead-time
1 thru 11	Improvements in all defined performance measurements are required

The first step in beginning the Lean Roadmap process is to develop a lean organizational structure: Building Block 1.

The following overviews are intended to convey the basics of the building block process and are covered in greater detail in Parts II through V.

Building Block 1 Overview: Lean Organizational Structure

The beginning point for the lean organizational structure is to link the Lean Roadmap building block processes with specific positions/people in the organization.

Benefits realized in linking Lean Roadmap Building Blocks to the organizational chart:

■ Responsibility for leadership in the design and implementation of each Lean Roadmap business process is focused.

■ Implementation across the plant/business is consistent/standardized in design.

■ There is one primary resource to contact for information, procedures, and training, though naturally other people in the organization also become proficient in the process.

■ Each business process team leader selects members of the team based on a cross-functional organizational basis determined by ownership of the business process.

The team members will be trained in Lean Roadmap design using a "learn and do" approach. The teams will:

1. Formalize performance measurement values for both the current state and future states of the business as required.
2. Map the current state value streams; quantify value added and non-value added costs.
3. Design a future state value stream flow for material and information.
4. Quantify the future state expectations, cost, quality, and productivity.
5. Present to management the current costs, planned costs, cost to implement, and the time required to implement.
6. Implement the Lean Roadmap building block processes.

Typical Lean Roadmap Organizational Assignments & Responsibilities

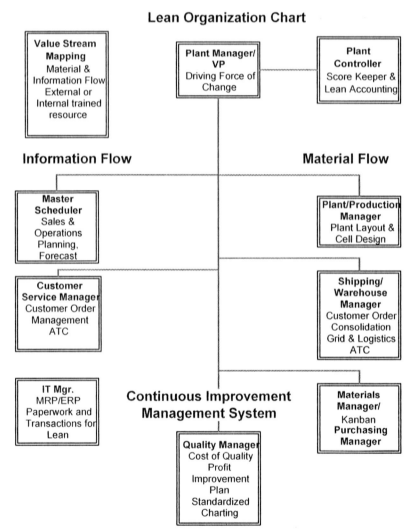

Figure 11: Lean Organization Chart

Building Block 2 Overview: Business Performance Measurements

Performance measurements are the basis for changing/improving your business, and are the common rallying point for determining over time your progress against the current value and the planned future state value.

Prior to embarking on a lean implementation, the company must define those business performance measurements that are targeted for improvement, and make certain that the teams understand and agree with the measurements—their importance, how they are calculated, and how they are displayed.

Current state measurements are easily defined at this time; and after you have completed detail mapping and quantifying of Lean Roadmap building block processes, the future state planned performance measurement goals will be defined. You'll need to develop performance measurements both at the plant level and at the cell level. Be selective in determining your key performance measurements; the fewer and more meaningful the better.

Performance measurements to consider are:

Those that impact the *customer* directly:
1. Quality
2. On-time delivery to the customer
3. Reduced lead time

Those that impact *shareholders*:
1. Cost of quality, warranty, scrap, quality department wages/fringes, (*Note: The first-pass yield of a value stream must be addressed and improved as required prior to coupling operation process steps.*)
2. Eliminate/reduce finished goods inventory, measured in turns or days, net of obsolete
3. Assemble/make to customer order
4. Return on assets
5. Floor space required

Those that affect **suppliers:**
1. Supplier 1-line MRP planning report
2. Consignment inventory
3. Supplier lead time
4. Those that affect **employees:**
5. Increase productivity, direct, indirect, and salaried
6. Kanban
7. Cross-training, and pay for skills.

Sample Performance Measurement: Customer On-Time Delivery

A typical business performance measurement chart (plant level) consists of the improvement target, how the performance is measured, and the calculation; a chart of actual to plan, and when plan is not met, the problem statement, root cause, and countermeasures to be followed, and when. This chart is used at the plant level on a weekly or monthly basis. As we examine the frequency of events in any of the Lean Roadmap routes, the shorter the cycle and the more frequent the event, the more often performance is measured; for example, hourly cell output against Takt time goals for the day.

Performance Measurement--Customer On-Time Delivery

ISSUE: Customer Service

Improvement Target	Measure
Reach on-time delivery of 92% by year end	Ratio of shipped complete on time to total orders shipped
2	

Problem Statement
Critical part from supplier not available #acr87f-4
4

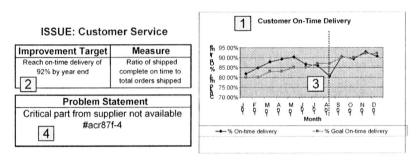

Root Causes	Countermeasures	Responsibility	Date
Supplier not notified of the change planned in a sales promotion	S&OP to recalculate & supplier 1-line planning report issued each time a major change in sales is identified	Bill SCM	Aug-01
5			

Figure 12: Performance Measurement

1. The plant measurement is clearly defined
2. Shows how the measurement is calculated
3. Shows the last reading and run time chart of progress
4. Shows what caused the goal for the period not to be achieved
5. Shows root causes, countermeasures, who and when.

Benefits of Defined Performance Measurements

▇ The future-state goals are defined in terms of performance measurements. This allows for a Lean Roadmap design that will reach the goals.

▇ Performance measurements are a common rallying point for improvement.

▇ A good deal of lack of confidence is felt when management does not properly express the performance measurements—so do it correctly the first time.

Building Blocks 3-10 Overviews: Value Stream Mapping (VSM)

A **value stream** is defined as a detailed listing of all the process steps required for the manufacture of a specific planning family group of products, for both material and information flow through the factory processes.

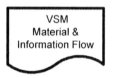

Value Stream Map (VSM) = the tracing of both material and information flow steps required to manufacture products contained in a planning family of products, assigning costs, time values, and value added or non-value added. Value Stream mapping is the one significant addition to the Toyota Production system of Just in Time, and is the core of Lean. The VSM process is significant in that in a matter of several dedicated working days, a VSM team can map and quantify the current state processes, the future state processes, and determine current costs, projected savings, cost to implement, and implementation timeline. The focus of the Value Stream Mapping Process is on improvement of the critical performance measurements identified earlier.

Keys to a successful VSM outcome are:

■ Each team must include a seasoned VSM facilitator who has a vision of the future state potential. The facilitator(s) must be experienced in material and information flow in a lean environment.

■ The facilitators must be prepared to use a portion of each day to train the team members in lean concepts of: cellular 1-piece material flow, assemble to order, point of use inventory, kanban, Sales & Operations Planning/supply chain planning, Available to Capacity (ATC) scheduling at order entry, and bills of material and process routings with reduced levels of structure and process steps.

■ There must be a daily agenda with daily team-to-team out-briefings. The senior management person responsible for the outcome should be present for these briefings.

■ Performance measurements must be defined, team leaders selected, and team members selected.

■ The process must be compressed and focused to yield the best results in a short time frame.

Typical outputs from a successful VSM are current and future state:

■ Cost of quality, scrap, rework, and warranty

■ On-time delivery

■ Lead-times

■ Productivity

■ Non-value added costs and lead-time days

■ Inventory $, current and required

■ Floor plan and material flow expressed as a spaghetti diagram

■ Organization required to support the production, indirect and salaried

■ Information flow, sales and operations supply chain planning, customer order management, materials replenishment

■ Current and future state cost summary

■ Future state savings, cost to implement, and time line

Building Block 3 Overview: Product Planning Families

Identification of product planning families allows us to logically rearrange and group together the factory manufacturing steps according to product families. The rearrangement of process steps into logical cells reduces production lead-time, work-in-process inventory and finished goods inventory (short lead-times for final assembly of products to customer order), and productivity. Additionally grouping products by planning families significantly simplifies the ongoing supply-chain planning process required for establishing capacity levels required to match forecasted/actual customer demand, calculation of kanban levels, and supplier planning and management.

A **product process planning family** (or simply *planning family*) is defined by family design and commonality within the bills of materials for the family. Thus a planning family is a logical grouping of products the business sells, by:

- Function of the product,
- Design configuration, and
- Manufacturing process route, i.e., similarity of routing steps.

Let's take our hypothetical Paradise Products as an example. A manufacturer of yard and garden powered tools/appliances may manufacture the following lines of products:

- String Trimmers-gas
- String Trimmers-electric
- Lawn Mowers-gas
- Lawn Mowers-electric
- Riding Lawn Mowers
- Leaf Blowers-gas
- Leaf Blowers-electric
- Widgets

Grouping these lines of products into product planning families is fairly intuitive. A first-pass might group gas and electric leaf blowers into a single family of products. Upon further examination, we might discover significant differences between the products, such as a gas engine versus an electric motor. These differences will likely dictate **two product planning families**, due to the very different component structures and manufacturing resources required.

Leaf Blowers are logical product planning families for the sales, operations, and accounting organizations for financial planning purposes, and for the development of cellular material flow and simplified capacity planning.

Building Block 4 Overview: Product Planning Family Sales Forecasts

Once product planning families have been created, a sales forecast may be easily developed for each product planning family, as explained in greater detail in Part III of this book. The forecast output provides us with input to cellular design and floor plan concepts, and is defined in a two-level process called Product Process Quantity (PPQ). In Part IV of this book, the planning family forecast will provide us with several important outputs utilized in sales and operations planning and supply chain planning.

Building Block 5 Overview: Product Process Quantity (PPQ) Matrix

The PPQ (Product Process Quantity) is a matrix of the products you manufacture, the routing steps, and the hours required to build the products from a historical perspective or from a forecast based on historical data. This step of the Lean Roadmap process allows you to group process steps, and to identify the number of resources in machines/operators required to meet the sales demand forecasted by the planning family.

There are two levels to the PPQ process. The Level 1 PPQ process defines the final assembly and test resources and hours required of the planning family to meet the maximum monthly demand for product. These are the cells that assemble product to customer order.

The Level 2 PPQ defines the resources and hours required to configure internal manufacturing cells that supply the final assembly cells with materials and assemblies required to assemble the family products.

Constraints are identified at this time for both the final assembly cells and the internal supplier cells, and the required resources are identified to meet the forecasted maximum customer demand for each product family.

Notes: The customer demand rate is expressed as TAKT time and is defined as the drumbeat rate of demand for product being ordered by the customer. Takt time is the rate that products must be produced to meet customer demand. The calculation for the Takt time = the hours available per shift/day to produce product divided by the units required per shift/day by the customers. Resources required to meet Takt time = total standard time to produce 1 unit of product/Takt time. These calculations are defined in detail later in this book.

For those businesses with very obvious material flows, the PPQ is not required, as the flow is evident and not complicated.

Benefits of Defining Product Planning Families, Family Sales Forecasts, Planning Bills of Material, and PPQ s are:

▪ Product families are the basis for value stream mapping, which assigns value and waste to each operation step of the manufacturing process.

▪ The planning family forecast for the entire planning family of products requires only one monthly quantity for the family per monthly planning period. Using a planning bill of material (explained in Part III) produces a forecast for all manufactured and purchased material. This information is then used for supply chain planning and is critical for realizing lead-time reduction from suppliers.

▌ The planning family forecast is the input for the PPQ Levels. The PPQ' s define the resources in equipment and manning required for any specific or all product families, and are the basis for establishing cell designs for both the final assembly cells and the internal manufacturing cells that will supply the final assembly cells.

Now that we have an idea of the product planning families and the resources required to meet the maximum monthly forecasted demand levels, we are ready to value stream map each family of products and define a future state process flow.

Building Block 6 Overview: Cellular/Plant Layout

Once the Product Process Quantity (PPQ) and forecast by family have been determined, a rough-cut VSM floor plan for the facility can be developed.

Widgets Final Assy. Line

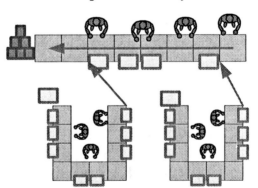

Widgets Sub. Assy. Lines

Figure 13: Widgets Final Assy. Line

Factors to consider in this phase are:

- Final assembly cells required
- Internal cells required to feed the final assembly cells
- Varying manning levels in cells based on customer demand using a simple TAKT time calculation
- Packaging at the cell
- Kanban and point of use material storage
- Cell/workstation layout
- Cell performance measurements and control of the improvement process by the cell associates

Benefits of cellular one-piece mixed model flow are:

- Reduced manufacturing lead time
- Reduced/eliminated finished goods
- Reduced scheduling complexity
- Reduced material moves
- Reduced floor space is required; generally by 30%-60%
- Productivity is increased by 20%-60% (Introduction of a continuous improvement process required.)
- Cell performance measurements are managed and improvement process controlled by the cell associates
- Cell associates manage the reorder of point-of-use inventory
- Cell associates handle the micro-scheduling of the cell

Building Block 7 Overview:
Sales & Operations Planning (S&OP)

Sales & Operations Planning

The Sales & Operations Planning process is designed to create and periodically update a common business plan across organizational functional boundaries. The plan for the foreseeable future, and in particular for the next month, is agreed upon by the operating groups. With a common plan, all groups within the business are concentrating their efforts on meeting and exceeding the common vision as defined in the S&OP plan.

Traditional S&OP processes fall short of meeting lean objectives in that the supply chain is managed by conventional MRP/ERP planning and/or building finished goods to forecast.

The Lean Roadmap process has improved traditional Sales & Operations Planning in numerous ways:

- Planning-family BOMs simplify the forecasting process, automatically calculating % planned for each member of the planning family.
- The forecast is used to manage the supply chain by:
- Using the forecast in units and capacity to notify suppliers on a weekly basis of booked/forecasted demand via a weekly supplier 1-line-per-part planning report
- Recalculation of kanbans based on the new plan
- Adjusting weekly capacity buckets at final assembly cells. This ATC function is embedded into the order entry process, and accurately books and schedules orders using a capacity based on units for one constraint within the final assembly cell. This process is explained in detail in following chapters.

**Sales & Operations Planning
Supply Chain Planning**

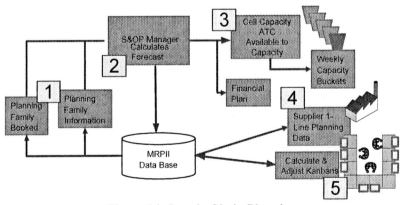

Figure 14: Supply Chain Planning

1. Product planning families are grouped into planning family bills of material, and a combination of history and market intelligence are used monthly to recalculate the sales forecast.
2. The sales forecast is calculated, as this business will no longer build finished goods to forecast. Material planning is simplified, as common material is consumed by planning family members.
3. An output of the forecast is the establishment of final assembly cell capacity measured in units of product. Weekly time frames of capacity are established in the order entry program, eliminating overbooking of capacity.
4. Suppliers are notified utilizing a simplified 1-line-per-item planning report, visibly showing in weekly and monthly increments, the planned requirements for each item purchased from the supplier. **Note: The first weekly period consists of booked customer order demand, and is often used as an automatic release of materials from suppliers. The report allows suppliers to adjust supply chain levels as required.**
5. All internal manufacturing cells are supplied electronically with a list of kanbans that have changed to a degree greater than a specific percentage/quantity. The kanbans are adjusted by the cell associates, and those that increased, triggering a reorder, are processed for reorder.

Benefits of a Lean Roadmap S&OP process:

- A cross-functional & shared business plan
- Final assembly capacity is defined for accurate scheduling at order entry
- Finished goods can be eliminated, given that the business chooses to assemble to customer order
- The financial plan is defined and agreed upon
- Suppliers are included in the supply chain management planning process

- Integrated planning process—simplified, and intended to adjust the supply chain inventory and capacity levels
- Reduced supplier lead times—they have a weekly plan. Lead time now equals transportation time
- Work-in-process inventory is significantly reduced
- Kanbans are recalculated and adjusted to meet the changing plan

Building Block 8 Overview :
Available to Capacity (ATC) Scheduling at Order Entry

The Available to Capacity (ATC) logic has one overriding benefit: *accurate scheduling of customer orders to available final assembly capacity.* The objective at order entry is to book an order, give an accurate delivery date for assemble/make to order, and achieve an outcome of assembling and shipping on time to the customer.

The Lean Roadmap process utilizes a proprietary process for doing this painlessly, utilizing your current MRP/ERP software. An outline of the process is as follows, and is detailed in Part V.

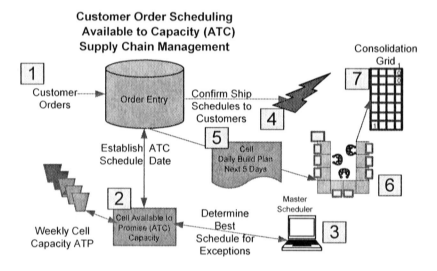

Figure 15: Customer Order Scheduling

1. Customer orders are received.
2. Each final assembly cell has a weekly capacity (ATC) expressed in units of product based on a weighted average time, yielding very accurate consumption of capacity. Weekly time buckets are used, as the purpose of the ATC logic is to macro-schedule the final assembly cell, and not overbook the capacity. The cell associates do the micro-scheduling to customer date. We do not consider material availability, as kanban material levels are calculated monthly along with cell ATC. This means supply chain capacity = supply chain demand at ATC. For non-repetitive items that are sold, the natural lead-time for the product is used and confirmed to the customer.
3. For customer orders where the capacity available is less than the customer demand, the master scheduler and customer service determine a best date with the customer.

4. Customer order confirmation acknowledgements are e-mailed to the customer shortly after the schedule date is determined.
5. A weekly/daily cell build schedule is reviewed daily by the cell team leader and a micro-schedule is determined. Manning/staffing levels for the next day/week are also determined to meet customer demand quantity and dates.
6. The final assembly cell builds the product and processes any required paperwork electronically, closes work orders, prints labels, packages.
7. Finished goods are delivered to the customer order consolidation grid by each cell multiple times per day, depending on volume.

Note: Always measure your performance to on-time delivery to the customer request date and to your promise date. The important date is the on-time shipment to the customer request date, as this relates to your ability to reduce lead-times and operate flexible assembly cells, moving resources from cell to cell to meet varying customer demands by product family.

Benefits of Available to Capacity (ATC) customer order scheduling:

█ Orders are easily scheduled in the background, to meet capacity without having to reschedule
█ On-time customer delivery is significantly improved, even considering that finished goods inventory has been removed
█ Fewer customer service representatives (CSRs) are required to field customer complaints regarding missed deliveries
█ Bills of material levels/work order levels are reduced
█ Routing steps are combined. Only the final assembly process is scheduled; all supplying operations are scheduled via kanban and build to order

■ ERP/MRP operations transactions are significantly reduced

■ A significant reduction in supporting overhead is required for scheduling, opening/closing work orders, picking material to order.

Building Block 9 Overview:
Customer Order Consolidation Grid Logic

The customer order consolidation grid logic is a process that eliminates the need to send finished goods to stores, store them, pick them again, and deliver them to shipping. As we are now manufacturing/assembling product to customer order date, product is being produced, picked up from several locations of manufacture/storage, and delivered to a specific collection point for delivery to the customer. Customers receive product by a delivery route method expressed as a specific freight carrier. The object is to consolidate all shipment items due out today in the appropriate grid (delivery route method/carrier). The savings in indirect warehouse costs are great, and this process supports the manufacture to customer order and short lead-time required for success.

The shipping/logistics manager determines the grids required and the size of each grid based on history, product size, and frequency of shipment.

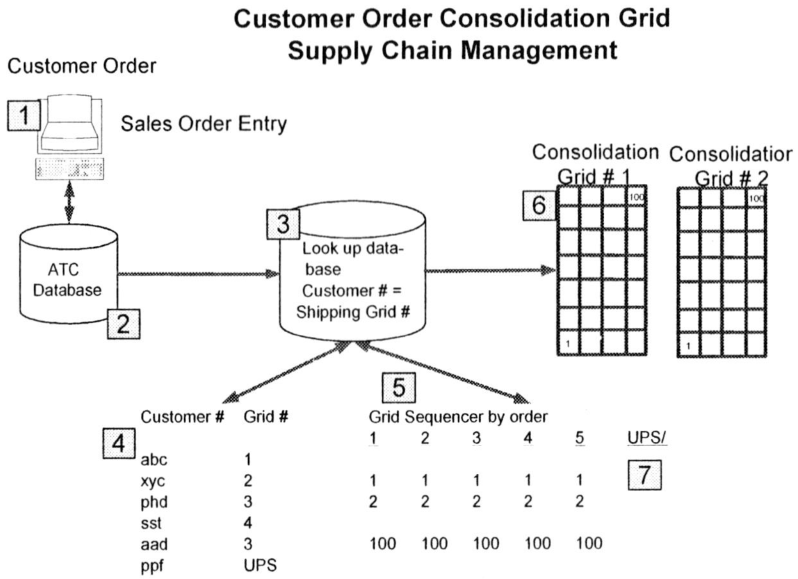

Figure 16: Customer Order Consolidation Grid

1. Customer orders are received.
2. The ATC schedule is determined.
3. The customer number is used to determine the consolidation grid collection point.
4. A customer # = grid #.
5. The location within the grid is determined by sequential selection. Note: A small business may have one grid per carrier route.
6. Product is produced and delivered to the grid, where it is checked against the customer order, and when complete is shipped.
7. For next-day delivery, the customer service representative can override the grid selection process and send the product to an overnight delivery point.

Benefits of utilizing a customer order consolidation grid:

■ The need to store finished assemblies is eliminated

■ The need to retrieve finished assemblies from racks is eliminated

■ The need to hunt, seek and retrieve finished goods is eliminated

■ The requirement for warehouse, space, racks, equipment, and people is reduced.

Building Block 10 Overview: Kanban

The kanban process is a natural and visual process of material replenishment for those items being consumed by the customers. Kanban quantities are recalculated monthly during the sales & operations planning (S&OP) process, and are adjusted to meet the changing forecast. Software is available to couple with your ERP/MRP business software for this purpose.

The reordering process is controlled by the cell associates for material that is stored at point of use. Given that the kanbans have been accurately calculated and the supply chain developed for this pull system, cell associates now manage the reorder process, and stock-outs drop significantly.

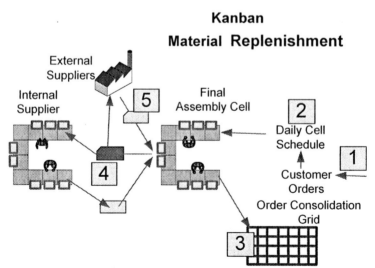

Figure 17: Kaban Material Replenishment

1. Customer orders are booked and ATC dates determined.
2. A weekly/daily cell schedule by ship date and quantity is updated and reviewed a least once daily. The cell leader determines the daily/weekly build schedule (micro schedule) and determines the required staffing level in the cell that is required to meet customer demand.
3. Product is built and delivered. As product is built, material stored in the cell in the form of kanban is consumed to build the product.
4. The cell orders material to replenish only that material consumed by the customer. Ordering of material is from internal and external suppliers.
5. Material ordered from cells is returned to a specific cell location, in the correct quantity and lead-time specified on the kanban card.

Benefits in utilizing a kanban process:

- Reduced inventory
- Point of use reduces indirect support
- Minimizes stock-outs at point of use
- "Pull" system of replenishment based on customer consumption of materials
- Shared "visual" system of inventory replenishment

VSM Summary: The Bottom Line

The output of the value stream mapping process is:

- *Employees who will enact a lean concept that they developed, believe in, and will play a key role in implementing*
- Current value stream costs
- Future/estimated value stream costs

■ Non-value added items identified for elimination/reduction
■ Cost to implement, capital & expense
■ Return on investment
■ Workplan steps and timing

The final step in the VSM baseline process is a presentation by the team members to the company decision makers—the ones who sanctioned the VSM process. As many team members as is possible and reasonable should make the presentation. This level of participation has a powerful impact on the decision makers.

Upon Completion of the VSM baseline study, the VSM teams established the above future state gains they believe are attainable. Please note that each improvement item has corresponding Lean Roadmap building block numbers assigned to indicate which steps are primarily responsible for the associated item improvement.

Lean Roadmap Building Block	Performance Measurement Widgets	Pre- Lean Roadmap Current State Value	Future State Value	Annual Savings/ income improvement
1, 2, 11	Quality Costs, Scrap, Warranty-Annual	$176,000	$50,000	$126,000
2, 3, 4, 5, 6, 7-9	On Time Delivery to Customers	53%	95% +	
2, 6, 8-11	Direct Labor Employees	42	36	$180,000
1-11	Indirect Labor Support	8	4	$120,000
1-11	Salaried Support	1	1	$0
3, 4, 6, 7, 8,10	*Inventory Finished Goods $	$3,475,346	0	$139,000
6, 10	* Inventory WIP $	$476,000	$42,000	$17,360
7, 10	* Inventory Raw $	$1,500,456	$600,000	$36,000
6, 10	Weighted Avg. Lead-Time Days Manuf.	27	2	
3, 4, 7, 10	Weighted Avg. Lead-Time Days Suppliers	58	5	
6	Distance Traveled to Make a Product	6500'	1245'	
6	Floor Space Value Added for Production	29500 sq ft	18100	
6, 9, 10	Floor Space Non-Value Added	45000 sq ft	5400	
6	Number of Operations to Schedule	12	1	
			Total *	$618,360

* inventory reduction annual income computed at 4% cost of money

Capital Cost to Implement			$78,000
Expense to Implement			$76,000

Future State Material Flow

Recall the original material flow for an electric leaf blower? The future state material flow is defined as:

■ Customer orders are scheduled at order entry utilizing ATC
■ The assembly schedule goes to the assembly and test cell for micro-scheduling to customer date
■ As products are assembled they go to a specific customer order consolidation point and are sent directly to the customer
■ As point of use material is consumed in final assembly and test, replacement kanban material is ordered from suppliers both internal and external

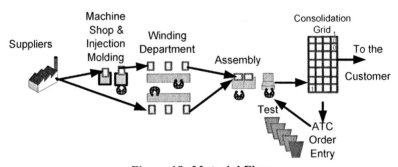

Figure 18: Material Flow

The Lean Roadmap process steps we used to develop our Lean Vision were:

■ Lean organizational structure was developed
■ Performance measurement categories were established
■ Product planning Families were defined
■ A planning family forecast was developed for both cell design and for supply chain planning, and for management

▪ A formalized value stream mapping event (**VSM**) was completed for both information and material flow.

Material Flow

▪ A PPQ matrix for all manufactured parts was developed, giving us the logic for grouping process steps in material flow.

▪ Based on the floor plan and final assembly cells/schedule points:

▪ The future state floor plan was developed in scope for simplified material flow.

▪ The kanban supermarket/storage points were located on the floor plan.

▪ Current state performance measurements were quantified based on the VSM process.

▪ The future state performance measurements were estimated.

▪ Savings and cost to implement were estimated.

▪ A timeline for implementation was developed.

▪ The plan was presented to senior management by the VSM team(s).

Information Flow

▪ The sales and operations planning process was developed, giving us key outputs for kanban, supplier planning, and ATC cell planning for order entry.

▪ The customer order management process, available to capacity (ATC), was implemented. This process matches customer demand to capacity and alerts order entry when capacity is exceeded. This process without failure improves on time delivery to the customer.

▪ The customer cell build plan was implemented, supplying the cell with a build plan based on customer date and cell capacity.

▪ The customer order consolidation grid logic was mapped.

▪ A kanban process was defined.

Building Block 11 Overview:
Continuous Improvement Management System

In our final building block, we design a Continuous Improvement Management System that is a closed loop process consisting of:

- Performance measurements
- Data collection
- Root causes defined
- Corrective/counter measures defined
- Implementation
- Data collection

The Continuous Improvement Management System is the basis for continuing improvement after implementation of a cell and for preventing a cell from sliding back into poor performance.

The process is effective when managed at the point of activity and measurement, such as a manufacturing cell. A properly designed process removes bureaucracy, and places control at the proper point in the process.

Parts II-V of **Lean Roadmap** explain in detail the Eleven Building Blocks of Lean Roadmap, and are intended for use by the VSM Lean Roadmap supply chain design teams.

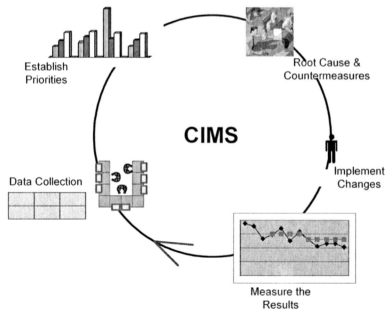

Figure 19: CIMS

PART II
MANAGEMENT AND THE
LEAN ORGANIZATION STRUCTURE

Employees as Part of the Lean Process

Leadership

A successful lean implementation requires leadership from the top down—consistent, focused management commitment and participation. In the successful implementation I have personally witnessed, I have identified six distinct characteristics that contributed directly to the success of the implementations: vision, a plan, confidence, organization and people skills, commitment, and integrity.

Vision

Performance measurements will be defined in a subsequent chapter. Suffice it to state here that the business leader must have a clear vision of the changes required and how they are to be measured. The leader must then clearly communicate the expected changes and their magnitude to everyone in the business.

A key to communicating a lean vision is to ensure that the changes that take place over time are recorded and displayed by the process owners, with a frequency that matches the rate of the work being done. As an example, book to bill may be daily and cost of quality monthly.

Vision is defined in measurable business metrics that support the continued success of the enterprise and the people who work there. These areas of improvement fall into three broad categories:

- Incremental and targeted sales increase at a target margin
- Cost reductions for current P&L items
- Asset management, including those items that are included in the balance sheet, such as inventory, and bricks-and-mortar (buildings)

Profit improvement and asset management improvement are planned events that never end in the lean business. At this moment in time, does your business have time-phased profit and asset improvement plans that support business performance measurements? These should include:

- Time-phased sales profit improvement plan
- Time-phased cost reduction plan
- Asset management plan
- Plant performance measurements
- Cellular performance measurements

A Plan

Business leaders who think in terms of business processes and of the improvement of these processes from beginning to completion, utilizing improvements that categorize the improvement potential and remove wasteful steps and non-value added costs. A plan for the improvement of critical business processes will ultimately result in quantum improvements for their business.

Processes that are vital to a successful lean business plan include:

- Value stream mapping
- Material flow concepts of cellular 1-piece mixed model flow

- Kanban
- Sales & operations planning
- Customer order scheduling at the time of booking
- Supply chain management
- Set-up reduction
- Continuous Improvement Management System
- New product introduction
- Acquisitions

Process is the means to improvement. Commencing with performance measurements, a value stream mapping baseline and future state, an implementation plan, and the use of sustaining processes of continuous improvement, will yield success.

Confidence

It takes confidence to lead a lean transformation. Not only are you faced with managing the business, you have customers, boards of directors, shareholders, employees, suppliers, and creditors to satisfy. Now you are taking on the additional challenge of changing the business processes to make them simplified and cost-effective.

Leaders with confidence and the courage to forge ahead are always armed with a vision and a plan, one that utilizes proven closed-loop improvement—processes guaranteed to significantly improve business performance. Another major source of confidence in successful leaders comes from their experience in working with others in a non-confrontational cooperative style, one that seeks the ideas and input of others. If your peers and employees trust you, they will not let you make a mistake that threatens the business.

The ability to proceed with confidence rather than fear is grounded in careful planning, experience, inclusion of others, and the capability to measure the progress and make changes midstream as required.

Organization & People Skills

The company's employees are a vital component and perhaps the most important element of a successful lean transformation. Change requires both leadership at various levels of the business, and inclusion of the people whose work will be changed. To elaborate on these two points I offer the following advice.

Lean Leadership Team

I urge you to develop a lean organizational chart for change management. (This concept is covered in detail in the following section of the book.) Once you have the lean organizational chart generically defined, select current employees to fill these important positions. Assess the capability of each person selected as a possible lean leader, and assess the likelihood of success against specific criteria.

When necessary, make the surgical changes called for to successfully manage the change that is required. Not all managers who are incumbents are willing or able to lead, plan, communicate, and facilitate change, nor are they able to rally support, cooperation, and enthusiasm.

People Skills

I cannot overstress the importance of treating people in the organization with respect and inclusion. Expedience, as a way of getting there faster, is a death knell when substituted for time that should be devoted to working with other employees, envisioning the future, and planning for change. I have witnessed both styles of management, and the outcome is always predictable. The leader who takes the time with each process team affected by the change, who explains the need and magnitude of change required, who describes the current process and seeks input for development of the future process, who plans and describes the steps for smooth implementation, will nearly always meet with success.

The people you work with have a vested interest in participating and assuring a successful and beneficial change, and will work to make the process work and improve over time. The expedient style almost always meets with failure and a good deal of frustration.

Commitment

The successful leader is committed to stay the course from the onset of a lean transformation through to the vision fulfillment and beyond. This commitment means active engagement in the plan through measurement, change management, communications, and time.

Integrity

There is no substitute for honesty when leading a lean transformation. As each Value Stream Mapping is completed and waste is eliminated, there is an obvious need for fewer people to complete the work. This can create stress and fear among employees. The best way to handle this is to introduce the lean process to employees and tell then that the process means change, and that some of that change may require a reduction in workforce.

Explain as well that some, and perhaps all, of the reductions can be compensated for by attrition, and expected sales increases as the company improves, having the shortest lead-time and best overall response to customer needs and requirements.

Building Block 1: Lean Leader Organization Structure Chart

The lean organizational structure addressed at this point entails the selection of specific people by company/plant location who will be assigned the task of defining a consistent and effective closed-loop lean process company/plant wide for each major building block process of the lean transformation. I will note here that the initial value stream mapping baseline process defines current and future state values at a high level, indicating:

- Costs and wastes
- Savings
- Cost to implement
- Timetables to implement

The lean leader organization chart defines those individuals who will detail current and future design of specific targeted processes required to complete the lean transformation. The individual assigned will lead a cross-functional team as required and define the objectives, process steps current and future, savings, costs, and implementation timetable, and will maintain an agenda, reporting on progress with timely and routine frequency.

While the need to define this lean structure may seem trivial or obvious, it is not. Successful results are for the most part relative to clear definitions of the process leader, the process itself, the deliverables, the support team, and the progress to plan.

In the typical functional, product-specific organizational structure, basic lean designs for cells, kanban, continuous improvement, supply chain management, and other processes sometimes are designed several different ways and lack consistent and well defined parameters of design, implementation, training, ongoing improvement, and reporting. This is what lean is designed to eliminate. However, we tend to revert to our learned management skills, and add waste to waste, if we do not examine the simplicity that is at our fingertips.

The following chart demonstrates the major elements of lean in organization chart format, and is presented as a guide.

Remember, the reasons for implementing lean are:

- Improve customer on-time delivery

- Reduce costs, both in manufacturing the part and in the overhead required to support operations
- Inventory reduction

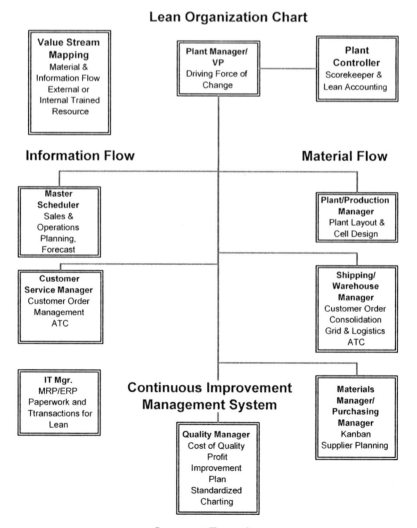

Lean Organization Chart

Value Stream Mapping
Material & Information Flow External or Internal Trained Resource

Plant Manager/ VP
Driving Force of Change

Plant Controller
Scorekeeper & Lean Accounting

Information Flow

Material Flow

Master Scheduler
Sales & Operations Planning, Forecast

Plant/Production Manager
Plant Layout & Cell Design

Customer Service Manager
Customer Order Management ATC

Shipping/ Warehouse Manager
Customer Order Consolidation Grid & Logistics ATC

IT Mgr.
MRP/ERP Paperwork and Ttransactions for Lean

Continuous Improvement Management System

Materials Manager/ Purchasing Manager
Kanban Supplier Planning

Quality Manager
Cost of Quality Profit Improvement Plan Standardized Charting

<u>Support Functions</u>
IT MRP/ERP Lean
Industrial Engineering Standardized Work
Maintenance/Plant Engineering Equipment Moves
Accounting Lean Costing
Engineering Standardization, Bills of Material
MRP/ERP Data Base Accuracy
Configure MRP/ERP for Lean

Figure 20: Lean Organization Chart

An explanation of the lean leader organization chart is in order. **Lean Roadmap** defines three primary processes required for successful implementation of lean: Information Flow, Material Flow, and a Continuous Improvement Management System. (The specific lean process design steps will be covered in detail later in this book.) In brief:

Information Flow, better known as the Supply Chain Management information process, is critical to a successful lean implementation. The information flow process that we have developed allows a business to take the current MRP/ERP business system and convert it to basic 101 lean. The information flow processes detailed later in this book are comprised of several Supply Chain Management components:

- Sales & Operations Planning
- ATC customer scheduling at order entry
- Customer order consolidation grid
- Kanban, material replenishment

Material Flow is the physical design of the shop floor with regard to cells, 1-piece mixed model flow, and pull replenishment of materials.

Continuous Improvement Management System is the closed-loop business process that assures continued improvement in the above processes.

Value Stream Mapping (VSM)

The introduction of this process has significantly improved the transformation process to a lean, just-in-time status in several distinct aspects.

Value Stream Mapping Material & Information Flow

- The VSM baseline current- and future-state process yields a high level plan for lean transformation for an entire factory. The entire high-level future-state plan takes only several days to develop.

(The time required in days will vary depending on the size and complexity of the factory and product families.)

■ The process yields these results as a product of a team effort, and the output is presented by a group of employees who firmly believe in the savings and timing presented. They form the basis for an implementation team.

■ The value stream is mapped for both material and information flow. Generally, mapping the flow for information is required only one time for a plant location, and for all plants located in a global region, as this is a common process. For material flow, a VSM is completed for each major product family.

■ A presentation by the VSM teams to senior management is a powerful, compelling, and convincing process that almost always achieves approval and buy-in.

The VSM process is a keystone process, and determines the direction and vision for the lean transformation. Therefore you'll want to carefully select team leaders for both information and material flow. Should you not have an experienced VSM mentor for a process, then go externally and get one who is qualified for each process.

Note: As a word of caution, my experience has been utter disappointment when looking for experienced mentors for information flow. The mentor has the important tasks of educating the team in lean and leading the team to quantum leaps of improvement. This requires a person who can envision a significantly improved future state and mentor the team out of the traditional processes and into the lean ones.

Information Flow Leader, Sales & Operations Planning

Master Scheduler Sales & Operations Planning, Forecast

The Sales & Operations Plan detailed later in the book is the key process for supply chain management and order fulfillment. So if you want to eliminate/reduce finished goods and accomplish most of the other lean benefits, this position is crucial. The person requires knowledge and credibility. Generally, the plant master scheduler knows the product families, manufacturing processes, key customers, and key managers, such as the plant manager, controller, sales manager, etc. The master scheduler is also a logical person to develop the forecast in units by family/value stream. When you consider that a good prediction of future sales can be developed by understanding recent sales and bookings, a sales forecast is not complicated to do. What is needed from the sales manager, that the Master Scheduler likely does not have is current and relative market intelligence, "tell me what I do not know," such as planned sales promotions, sales channel changes, and new product introductions.

Customer Service Manager Customer Order Management ATC

The **Lean Roadmap** process for Customer Order Management **Available to Capacity (ATC)** is unique, simple, and effective. Imagine a process for customer order entry that schedules a customer order for delivery, and a supporting lean process that delivers product on time to the promised date. Development of this process and integration into your current MRP/ERP process is simple and rewarding to both the customer service group and the customers, and also to manufacturing, as the Lean Roadmap process consumes capacity available. The **Customer Service Manager** will develop this process and drive implementation.

IT Mgr. MRP/ERP Paperwork and Transactions for Lean

The **IT Manager** must manage the task shared by users of the Information Flow **MRP/ERP** process: database clean-up and configuration for lean. Unfortunately, I have seen more failed MRP/ERP implementations than successful ones. Failed implementations occurred because there was no **Lean Roadmap** information flow defined for configuration of the software or for its use after implementation. Secondly, the pre-lean implementation database is generally corrupt with inaccurate information, such as inventory, lead times, and bills of material. This poor situation was not all bad years ago, when your competitors were as poorly structured as you may be today, but the good old days of being able to tolerate this kind of waste (which, by the way, requires tremendous support services) are gone. The first competitor who adapts to lean will increase profit margins without increasing prices.

Material Flow Leader

> Plant/Production
> Manager
> Plant Layout &
> Cell Design

The **Plant or Production Manager** oversees the design of the factory floor, from high-level material flow concepts developed in the value stream mapping exercise, down to the cell design steps and concepts. The material flow and cell design affects most of the employees who work in the to-be cells, and the support people who maintain and service the cells. The current Plant Manager is a logical choice to lead this effort, as that person has the most to gain by a properly designed flow, and the most to lose by one that is not properly conceived.

Design of the flow of material requires cross-functional inputs of materials, receiving, shipping, cell leaders, supervision, etc. The cell design requires the input and participation of employees working the process. Concepts of 1-piece flow, material stored at point of usage, kanban, set-up reduction, 5S, and performance measurements need to be understood by people working in the cell; and when it comes to station layout, the employees doing the work are a valuable asset and resource to assist in the cell design.

Shipping/ Warehouse Manager Customer Order Consolidation Grid & Logistics ATC

Design and implementation of the **Customer Order Consolidation Grid** is a key building block in removing non-value added overhead in warehousing. This process moves product directly from the assembly department to a specific spot in shipping that is the consolidation point for that order, and is also the grid that consolidates all orders that will go outbound via that shipping route. At the time an order is booked, the grid is assigned, and all labels used in the assembly process point to the correct grid location for consolidation. Imagine eliminating storage racks and the associated finished goods inventory, lift trucks, labor wasted in storage and retrieval from racks, on and on. The current **Shipping Manager** understands the current shipping routes, shippers, labeling, boxing, customer preferences, etc., and is usually the best person to design this process. You will need additional assistance from your IT group to add the logic to the order entry process.

Materials Manager/ Purchasing Manager Kanban Supplier Planning

Kanban & Supplier Planning/Management is a cornerstone of materials replenishment, and is the basic process for reordering material that the customer is consuming, instead of ordering material you think the customer may order. The reorder process is managed/triggered by the people assembling the product and consuming materials in the manufacturing process. In a standard MRP/ERP process, a message triggers telling a planner to order material; however, items such as substitution, scrap, and rework (common in non-lean environments) often are not accounted for, leading to inaccurate inventory and untimely reordering. The employees making the product want a better process for assuring availability of material. The kanban process does this, if properly designed, implemented, and maintained. This should be a joint purchasing/manufacturing planner development process. As only one or two people are assigned the development and implementation task, again we achieve a consistent process.

Quality Manager
Cost of Quality
Profit
Improvement
Plan
Standardized
Charting

Continuous Improvement Management System (CIMS) The CIMS process is a closed-loop process of waste identification, root cause, and corrective action implementation designed to assure continued improvement in all primary processes. The **Quality Manager** is responsible for the cost of quality, and is the coordination point for development of a CIMS process, with focus on the critical few, and coordination with the operating functions, both at a plant level and at a cell level.

Plant
Controller
Score Keeper &
Lean Accounting

The **Plant Controller** has an essential role in the development of a **lean accounting process**. Several areas of participation and or leadership come to mind.

1. Certifying the results of any value stream mapping process, both the current state and the future state values for improvement. This participation gives credibility to the teams' efforts.
2. Lean implementation and continuous improvement auditing to certify results of implementation over time.
3. Lean accounting has several benefits that can be derived in the transaction processes, such as labor reporting/work orders, labor variance reporting, WIP inventory transactions, and purchase order transactions. This in no way abrogates our responsibility for accurate accounting and reporting; rather it reduces the number of transactions required.

■ **Labor reporting/work orders.** The physical establishment of manufacturing cells requires that the bills of material levels be reduced (flattened) utilizing phantom structures in the bills of material. For every manufacturing assembly that becomes a phantom, a MRP/ERP work order is eliminated; this means that the opening and closing of the work order is not required. Labor reporting in a cell requires only a measurement of standard hours earned to standard hours paid. The cell leader utilizes a table that lists the part/assembly number and the standard hours per unit. At the end of the shift, a simple calculation of hours earned divided by total hours paid for the cell is done.

■ **WIP inventory transactions.** In lean we use a process called, in MRP/ERP verbiage, "backflushing." As material finished goods are received into finished goods inventory, they are backflushed, which means that all BOM standard labor, associated overhead, and direct material is applied to finished goods. In a traditional sense of production, a work order is opened for a manufactured part/assembly, material is issued as WIP, labor is applied, and part/assembly is produced and received into inventory. In backflushing, there are no WIP transactions required. The reason we can accept this is:

1. Lean times have been reduced to hours or days.
2. Kanbans and reduced lead-time have increased WIP turnover.
3. An accounting figure for WIP value is used based on the business level in sales and the product mix.

■ **Purchase order transactions.** Lean utilizes supplier 1-line MRP planning and kanbans, plus blanket order contracting, which defines terms, conditions, and legal commitments and does not commit the company to a long-term financial obligation. We can then define how we will be committed for purchase releases and how we pay the supplier for goods received. The individual supplier obligation can be a simple agreement to commit to a specified period of commitment based on the supplier 1-line planning report. Payment for goods can be done based on shipments made by the suppliers to kanban, release from consignment, or products you ship to customers.

■ **Labor variance reporting.** As we all know from experience, this process can be a pleasant event displaying progress and improvement against a VSM future state process followed by a continuous improvement process, or it can be a brutal, confrontational, and adversarial event repeated each month, with each of us preferring reasons that unplanned events created problems. More often than not we simply cannot trace the reasons for variance, and frankly who cares? What we want is a process of improvement and a look to the future.

The plant controller should encourage a process of reporting only finished goods completion from the final assembly cell. The supplying cells are continually making kanban replenishments; finished goods are backflushed. Additionally this person must insist on a continuous improvement process that is real and performance measurements that are posted: daily and weekly.

```
Plant Manager/
      VP
Driving Force of
    Change
```

The **Plant Manager, VP Operations, General Manager**, is the driving force of change. Specific responsibilities were covered earlier in the Leadership section. The incumbent will oversee the lean implementation from vision to completion. Specific measurements begin at the vision stage and are quantified in the value stream mapping process. The incumbent will be engaged in the profit improvement process, working capital reduction in inventory, improved customer service and quality levels, and will maintain a focus on those items that are critical to improving the business.

Lean implementation will achieve most/many of the gains to be achieved; however, without a standardized closed-loop CIMS and visual hourly/daily/weekly measurements, the process begins to digress and lose the gains achieved.

Management & the Lean Organization Chart

As managers and leaders at your company, you have a wonderful opportunity to be wildly successful implementing a lean roadmap at your business. The primary keystone to building a lean organization is in the selection of the most talented, creative, energetic people in the organization. I have witnessed and experienced the power and rate of momentum that is achieved when the best people are selected, organized, and focused on improvement. Not only do they perform their assigned tasks, they also make significant contributions to creative process design and implementation. As a manager and leader, the same old process of overtaxing the few who always get these assignments must now include as many more of the total employment as is required to reach critical mass and momentum.

As team leaders select team members, a great opportunity awaits those leaders with enough energy to tap into this pool, select the people, provide the "Learn & Do" training method of implementation, and watch the results.

One less-discussed significant benefit to this process is derived from the low cost, high impact solutions that result from accepting input from people who have worked their lives "doing more with less." Or we could turn this over to those who create solutions from afar—we all have experienced those helpful designs and ideas.

Employees: Junior Industrial Engineers at Large

We can look around us, as the Lean Roadmap teams proceed through the VSM baseline process, and on into the detailed Lean Roadmap design and implementation, and lo and behold, as the process of discovery, development, and implementation unfolds, we find that we have discovered a cadre of junior industrial engineers in our own midst.

It makes no difference which part of the material or information flow is being developed for implementation. When we take the time to engage the employees who currently work the process, seeking to learn about more creative and less costly ways of doing a job, those people invariably rise to the occasion by further defining the process and developing methods and creative solutions for further improving the process. Please keep in mind that 30%-60% improvement in shop and front office productivity results from a Lean Roadmap implementation. These junior industrial engineers give us something that no trained engineer may be able to provide us: *a process guaranteed to work.* Our employees have to work with the new lean process, and they will not let us do anything that makes little sense or that makes their work harder than they currently suffer. Therefore, given that we allow participation and respect input from the team, we will unleash our junior industrial engineering team.

Assessing the Lean Leader Knowledge Level

It is a valid and required step to assess the knowledge level of the team leaders with respect to the lean organization chart and Lean Roadmap module they will have responsibility for developing and implementing. The two aspects of assessment are:

- Leadership
- Lean Roadmap module knowledge

Each team leader must be assessed for the purpose of determining current knowledge levels and need for training to assist the team leader in successfully completing the assignment.

Leadership

The team leader needs to be a person who is knowledgeable in the assigned module, respected by associates, and possesses the characteristics to lead, listen, and communicate with others. The team leader:

- Accepts responsibility for the outcome
- Selects team members
- Takes the initiative
- Establishes performance measurements for the team
- Establish a visual measurement of progress

■ Schedules a routine time to meet and review progress with the team

■ Uses a formal workplan schedule with dates and names

■ Interfaces frequently with team members to support progress and provide proper mentoring

Lean Roadmap Knowledge

Knowledge of Lean Roadmap elements in the assigned module is generally present in the current state process. However, the actual VSM process will reveal many procedural steps that are not known by the leader. The difficulty lies in being able to envision a Lean Roadmap future state. Although this book certainly gives team leaders a basis for development of a lean future state process, it is a good idea to hire an external resource to mentor the teams during the VSM and implementation process.

Assessment of leaders can be determined by utilizing a written questionnaire such as the following example, with the questions being limited in number and focused on the area of responsibility. I prefer a written questionnaire, where the team leader responds with a written response, and a flow chart of the future state process.

Sample Assessment Form:

| Company Name | Date |
| Your Name | Title |

This questionnaire is a tool to determine your Lean Processes knowledge level. Based on your responses, we are better prepared to seek training and assistance for you as the assignment and deliverables of improvement required are defined.

Instructions

For each topic, give a written answer that covers three items:

- Your e Your definition of the topic
- Experience in implementation
- A flow chart for the topic—how does it function

Example:

Kanban—Define a kanban process.
Definition
Experience
Flow Chart: Show the kanban replenishment and scheduling process for a purchased and manufactured item stored in an assembly cell.

Cellular One-Piece Flow—Define the steps for designing a workcell
Definition
Experience
Flow Chart: Select a typical product we assemble and draw a flow chart for material flow through the cell.

Building Block 2: BusinessPerformance Measurements

Performance Measurements are vital to success and have a place in every business. The measurements are developed by management and team leaders, and a baseline measurement is defined at the VSM event. Also at the VSM event, a future state goal is defined for achievement.
Now, I want you to answer a very important question. When performance measurements are asked for, who is being measured? For those of you who answered the employees, you are incorrect. **The performance measurements measure management.** Let us examine this statement and see if we can agree on a number of points that may help clear up the reason I say we are measuring management.

1. Management, not the employees, developed the processes and methods that employees work within.

2. There are no bad employees. Every employee comes to work each day with a desire to do a good job. It does not always turn out that way because of poor methods and processes.
3. Employees working in the methods and processes have little authority to change a process. (I am talking about a total process, not a minor step in the process.)

Employees are paid to do a good job to the best of their ability. Once performance measurements are implemented, we can also ask those same employees to collect data that, once catalogued in Pareto and run chart format, will tell the management team what items to focus on for improvement. We can also ask employees to manage the Continuous Improvement Management System (CIMS) process for the area or cell they work within. However, it is up to management to develop the CIMS and oversee its validity and accomplishments.

Do not measure employees unless you have made a commitment to support the improvement process by introduction of a closed-loop continuous improvement management system.

Do not focus on productivity, but do measure it. As the non-value added waste in the process is eliminated, the productivity will improve without focusing on it.

Continuous Improvement Management System (CIMS)

In every business, the lack of continuous improvement simply means that continuous dis-improvement is occurring. The CIMS is the basis for managing ongoing improvement beyond the initial Lean Roadmap implementation components, which yield significant improvements. A very basic process of data collection, prioritizing of improvement potential, root cause determination/problem solving, and implementation of counter measures is required.

Establish a CIMS, built around:

■ Performance measurements, controlled at the point of measurement

■ A closed-loop process of waste identification and elimination based on performance measurements and data collection: Establishing priorities, identifying root cause of the problems/non-value-added determined, defining corrective actions/countermeasures, implementing changes, measuring the results

■ A process for improvement that reduces bureaucracy and communicates priorities for improvement to the entire workforce

■ A CIMS process that is management driven and supported

Should the performance measurements be at an assembly cell level, the employees need to be trained in the elements of CIMS. They should be given a list of technical support problem-solvers to call for assistance, and a frequent review of progress should be displayed on the cell run charts by plant management.

Cellular performance should be limited to quality, delivery, productivity (this will take care of itself with the elimination of non-value added), cross-training, and safety, and should be updated by the designated cell leader/associate. We are not looking for pretty computer-generated charts; we are looking for substance. When data is collected in a cell and an office worker takes the data away and creates a series of measurement charts, quite often the cell associates have difficulty in relating to the printed charts.

A typical CIMS system design and implementation should include the following steps:

1. Define the CIMS closed-loop process steps, including the closed-loop steps already defined, data collection and ongoing performance measurement charting, team structures for data collection and for problem solving (the technical support team).
2. Select an area to which to apply the CIMS steps.

3. Select a team leader. This should be the person from the process steps(s) being improved, such as a cell leader.

4. Determine training required in the tools of continuous improvement. A good deal of this training is available and can be located easily over the Internet. The important step in the process is the CIMS design.

5. Introduce the CIMS process to employees. The employees need to know that a process has been defined for improving the business. This process leads to increased profits for the business, job retention/creation, and an improved working environment for all. It is important to include a good cross-section of employees when the CIMS process is being designed.

Continuous Improvement Management System
Design and Implementation Steps

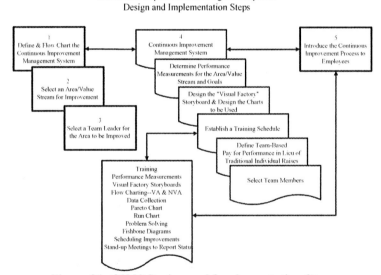

Figure 21: CIMS Design and Implementation Steps

The CIMS process steps are:

1. Data is collected pertaining to established performance measurements of quality, delivery, productivity, and non-value added wastes such as scrap, rework, waiting.
2. The cell leader updates a Pareto/bar chart, which will be used to establish priorities for improvement. The cell/process leader will engage the technical support team as required to assist in identifying root cause of non-value added waste and countermeasures required.
3. The technical support team member selected based on the top priority category item will develop root cause and countermeasure steps, either working with the cell employees or including other technical support as required.
4. Countermeasure changes are implemented as planned. Be sure urgent items are attended to immediately.
5. Data is continually collected and compares against last period data. I suggest you maintain a 4-week Pareto/bar chart of non-value added items by category and a 1-week Pareto/bar chart, and that they be compared to determine if improvements are actually being made. The cell point of data collection also needs to maintain a run chart of performance measurements to determine improvement over time.

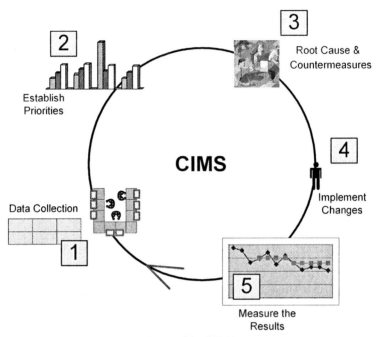

Figure 22: CIMS

When establishing the CIMS, consider establishing a two-level group structure of employees. The first group collects non-value added data and establishes priorities for correction and progress, such as assembly cells, and displays the results. The second group is the technical support team that determines root cause and countermeasures required to correct the problem.

PART III
VALUE STREAM MAPPING (VSM)

A *value stream map* is a quantified list of all the process steps taken to manufacture a family of products sold by the business. There are two distinct value stream maps: the *material flow* (supplier to manufacturer to distribution to the customer) and the *information flow* (from the customer to the distributor, manufacturer, supplier).

The major categories of quantification for each process step are: operation cost, lead-time required, floor space required, productivity, and inventory. Each process step is assigned a category: value added or non-value added.

The value stream mapping process requires an internal cross-functional team that selects an appropriate value stream (product family) for improvement and utilizes the VSM process to quantify the improvement potential. Essentially, we want a successful VSM study to indicate with assurance the potential improvement a business can expect to realize by implementing Lean Roadmap across a value stream product family, or across an entire manufacturing location/plant. The VSM must deliver:

- Current process steps and associated costs, lead-time, and inventory for the value stream.
- Future-state process steps and associated costs, lead-time, and inventory for the value stream.
- Cost of implementation.
- Time-line for implementation.

█ An internal cross-functional team of employees who have developed the VSM information, will make the presentation of findings to management, and will be members of the implementation teams.

█ Sufficient detail to support the planned future-state improvements, as certified by the plant controller.

The VSM process is time compressed and focused into a 6- to 10-day period of time, depending on complexity. Team members are relieved from normal duties and are focused on completing an intense:

█ Evaluation of the current process
█ Design of an improved process
█ Quantification of savings and cost to implement

Prior to starting the actual VSM process, it is beneficial to complete Lean Roadmap Building Blocks 3 and 4:

█ **Planning family identification**
█ Planning bill creation
█ Forecast for each product family

This information is used not only for the future-state supply chain design, but is also required for supply chain planning and management subsequent to lean implementation. **The importance of devoting sufficient time to these building block steps of Lean Roadmap cannot be overstressed.**

Building Block 3: Defining Product Planning Families

In Building Block 3 of Lean Roadmap, the company's products are grouped into families, based on geometry/bill of material similarity and manufacturing process similarity.

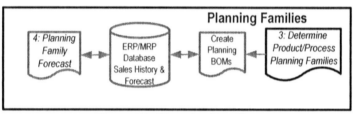

Figure 23: Planning Families

Grouping product families in lean is used for lean design, supply chain planning, and daily supply chain management. Families are used by operations to plan for staffing and for required direct materials. (The sales and accounting functions generally group broader families of product for purposes of financial budgeting and forecasting.) Determining product family groupings of products requires input and discussion by sales, operations, accounting and engineering.

Grouping families of product requires more than a simple grouping by name. The acid test for grouping resides in two factors: the bill of material content in terms of material required to build the product, and similar process steps required to build the product. The fact that sales items are named the same does not qualify them for grouping into the same family. For example, gas-powered leaf blowers and electric leaf blowers will likely require two separate groups.

Planning Family Bills of Material

The overall Lean Roadmap goal is to build/assemble product to customer order, meeting the customer request date. This requires timely supply chain planning and management to arrange for raw material and sub-assemblies quantities at strategic kanban locations and to replenish material as it is consumed by the customer.

A typical business selling many product variations finds the process of forecasting material and capacity difficult and time-consuming. Product planning family bills of material by family removes this difficulty.

The purpose of planning family bills of material is to simplify the forecasting process. This is done by grouping all family product models bills of material together under one family bill of material, and forecasting one quantity per month per planning family. At each forecasting session, the quantity or percentage forecast for each family member is calculated. The total of all family percentages equals 100% for the planning family.

	History Sold					
	O-03	N-04	D-04			
Planning Family Leaf Blowers Electric	20	18	24	Total Units Sold	% of Total Sold	Average/day sold
C3456	325	315	478	1118	35%	18
C3457	438	412	365	1215	38%	20
C3458	235	248	345	828	26%	13
Totals	998	975	1188	3161	100%	51
Average Units/Day	49.9	54.2	49.5	51.0		

Figure 24: Product Planning Chart

In the above example, the Product Planning Family Part # is **Leaf Blowers Electric** The total sales of the 3 models within the family was 3161 units for the last 3 months of time. The % of total sold is also the % for each model in the planning bill of material.

The next step in the process is the calculation of a family forecast for the planning family. The maximum monthly demand by family is used to plan cell capacity and design.

Building Block 4: Planning Family Product Sales Forecasts

Establishing a forecast utilizing product planning family logic is simplified as compared to traditional forecasting methods. The planning is accomplished using MRP/ERP business software, which is likely to be already running at your facility.

						Forecast			
[1]	**[3]**	**[4]**	**[2]**	**[5]**	May-04	Jun-04	Jul-04	Aug-04	Total
Total Units Sold	% of Total Sold	Average/ day sold	Planning Family Leaf Blowers Electric		20	**[6]** 25	19	20	84
1118	35%	18	C3456		433	541	411	433	1818
1215	38%	20	C3457		431	539	410	431	1811
828	26%	13	C3458		240	300	228	240	1010
3161	100%	51	Sales Forecast		1104	1380	1049	1104	4638
51.0			Average Units/Day		55.2	55.2	55.2	55.2	55

Figure 25: Product Planning Forecast Chart

As shown in the above diagram, a forecast for the Parent Family # **Leaf Blower Electric** creates a forecast for each of the planning family bills of material attached to the family #, and in the correct proportion. An explanation of the forecasting process is as follows.

1. Sales history for each planning family member is determined based on a range of history.
2. The planning family part/model # is displayed.
3. The % of the total units sold for the entire family is calculated. This % is used to calculated the forecast % for the future.
4. The average daily units sold is calculated. This is the total units sold for the historical period divided by the working/sales days for the period.
5. The forecast period months and working days per month are used to plan the forecast. A forecast for the

71

family is determined. A % increase or decrease for a planning family member is used for a final adjustment in situations where history is not available, such as a new product release.

6. A total adjusted forecast by month for each planning family is then used in the MRP/ERP software to calculate individual part number requirements.

It is important to understand that a forecast in the Lean Roadmap process is used to plan the supply chain materials and capacity required to support the forecast—not finished goods. This equates to planning kanban levels, supplier planning, and capacity planning for cells. As we are not building/assembling product to forecast, but rather populating the supply chain with material to allow for assembly to customer order, the forecast does not require modeling or simulations to be effective.

It is always prudent to over-plan somewhat for repetitive items. This does equate to somewhat higher kanban levels, which is a sound financial trade-off for finished goods inventory. Finished goods have labor overhead and material costs built into the inventory $. Raw/purchased materials have only the purchase cost and some small overhead $.

From this point forward, a generic product called Widgets will be used to demonstrate the power of the eleven building blocks of Lean Roadmap. The primary reason for using an unknown product called widgets is to assure that the readers focus on process steps, and not focus on a real product and how much better or worse your current cycle times are than if a specific product sample were to be used.

Building Block 5: PPQ: Product Process Quantity Matrix Manufacturing Cells Defined by Planning Family

The PPQ (Product Process Quantity) matrix is used to determine which work centers are required to produce a forecasted quantity of one or more product families. The PPQ is generally not required for simple and obvious manufacturing facilities; but for large, complex facilities it is a useful tool for simplifying plant layout and material flow.

The PPQ takes the guesswork and random opinions out of the cell development process and assures that a baseline identification of resources is available for use during the VSM process. This step significantly shortens the future-state concept development for material flow and cell development.

The PPQ process is a two level analysis process:

1. PPQ Level 1: Final Assembly Cells. This level utilizes the planning family forecast to determine the work centers/resources required for final assembly of planning family products. The final assembly cells are where customer orders are scheduled and built, matching capacity to demand.
2. PPQ Level 2: Internal Supplier Cells. This level is used to determine the manufacturing steps and resources required to develop cells that supply product to the final assembly cells. These cells are the sources of kanban replenishment for the final assembly cells.

PPQ Level 1: Final Assembly Cells

A search of MRP/ERP database history and forecast is used to develop the PPQ resources and time required to manufacture families of product. For example, the following illustration shows:

1. The list of products assigned to a product family.
2. The family name for the products and family designation,
3. The work center to which this product is routed and the total standard time required to produce the last 6 months of usage
4. The sales/usage of each product for the last 6 months
5. The total standard hours required for the last 6 months of production by family and work center

As shown, for the final assembly level of the electric leaf blower products, the work center's rotor assembly, field assembly, motor assembly/test, and final assembly test/pack are required.

Widget Final Assembly, Test & Package Cell

PPQ Level 1 Final Assembly Routing Sequence and Standard Cycle Time

Operation Work Ctrs	Step 1	Step 2	Step 3	Step 4	Step 5	Step 6	Total
Planning Family Widgets Set Up Hrs.	0.00	0.00	0.00	0.00	0.00	0.00	0.00
C3456 Cycle Times	35	32	34	30	36	32	199
C3457 Seconds	36	34	38	32	42	34	216
C3458	39	38	42	34	46	38	237
Weighted Avg Times	36	34	37	32	40	34	213
Forecasted Takt Time Seconds	9.08	9.08	9.08	9.08	9.08	9.08	
Stations Required	4.0	3.7	4.1	3.5	4.4	3.7	23.5

Figure 26: PPQ Level 1 Chart

PPQ Level 2: Internal Supplier Cells

As shown in the following illustration, PPQ Level 2 is a listing of resources required and the amount of time required to meet the forecast. For example, the following illustration shows:

1. The process steps in the manufacturing cell that are required to make a part used in the final assembly product widgets.
2. The part number required for the widget, and the cycle time for each step and part #.
3. The weighted average cycle time for the family of parts.
4. The forecasted Takt time for the aggregate family in the cell.
5. The number of stations/associates required to meet the forecasted Takt time for each operation.

		Step 1	Step 2	Step 3	Step 4	Step 5	Step 6	Total
Widget Sub Assembly Cell								
PPQ Level 2 Internal Supplier Routing Sequence and Standard Cycle Time								
[1] Operation Work Ctrs								
Planning Family Widgets	Set Up Hrs.	0.20	0.15	0.09	0.00	0.00	0.00	0.44
2342	Cycle Times	47	36	30	18	16	18	165
2345	[2] Seconds	44	38	36	20	18	20	176
2365		32	38	34	24	20	16	164
[3]	Weighted Avg Times	43	37	33	20	18	18	169
	Forecasted Takt Time	9.079	9.079	9.079	9.079	9.079	9.079	[4]
[5]	Stations Required	4.702	4.090	3.629	2.2031	1.935	2.011	18.569

Figure 27: Widget Sub Assembly Cell

As shown, for the widgets, the internal supplier cell(s) that will supply the final assembly cell(s) require a cell comprised of six distinct steps.

Having determined our Product planning Families, grouped them into planning bills of material, and used a forecast to obtain a PPQ, we have the information required for each family to trace the material flow through the business, and to assign measurements for each step in the process. We also have a good idea of the resources required to build manufacturing cells and the resources required to meet customer demand at peak demand. With this information in hand, the value stream mapping process can begin.

Value Stream Mapping Agenda: The Process in Detail

The following section outlines an agenda for conducting a successful VSM. The time and scope of the VSM is determined primarily by product planning family (value stream) breadth and complexity, and somewhat by the size of the facility.

The section will cover:

- A VSM Sample Product Family Overview
- A description of Performance Measurements to improve
- A Guideline for Team Selection
- A discussion of VSM Training, Preparation, Data Collection, and Assignments
- A description of Current State Material Flow Maps
- A description of Current State Information Flow Maps
- A section on Lean Roadmap Future State Training
- A section on how to quantify opportunities for improvement
- A section on Future State Process Maps
- A summary of Final Solutions and Major Improvements
- A discussion of the Implementation Plan and Management Presentation

VSM Sample Product Family Overview

The product family selected for the Lean Roadmap implementation is Paradise Products' widgets. Data collected reveals the following information from the Current State VSM:

- The widgets are a high end product sold to specialty shop and catalogue sales channels.
- The current plant layout for the product consists of final assembly stations, none of the stations are linked or coupled into cells Final widget products are made to forecast, this includes any sub assemblies required to make the final widget models. There is a warehouse and a packaging department.
- As customer orders are received, orders are picked from stores, packaged, and sent to customers.
- As stocked components and assemblies are consumed, buyers and planners issue additional work and purchase

orders based on forecast/customer order consumption of material.

■ The widget consists of parts and assemblies made by the company, and miscellaneous hardware and other purchased parts.

■ There are 3 models of widget offered for sale.

■ The plant averages 20 working days/month, 240/year.

■ Maximum daily forecasted demand is 2974 units.

■ Shifts worked at maximum demand = 1 shift and 7.5 hours of effective scheduled time/shift.

■ Current manning = 42 direct, 8 indirect, and 1 salaried.

■ Required Takt time = 9.08 seconds at maximum demand. (A widget is required to be assembled every 9.08 seconds to meet maximum monthly forecasted demand.)

■ Total direct labor standard time/unit = 213 seconds for the widget assembly, test and pack.

Performance Measurements to Improve

There must be a clear definition of desired improvements prior to beginning the VSM process. As the VSM is completed, values for each performance measurement are determined.

Performance Measurement Widgets
Quality Costs, Scrap, Warranty-Annual
On Time Delivery to Customers
Direct Labor Employees
Indirect Labor Support
Salaried Support
*Inventory Finished Goods $
* Inventory WIP $
* Inventory Raw $
Weighted Avg. Lead-Time Days Manuf.
Weighted Avg. Lead-Time Days Suppliers
Distance Traveled to Make a Product
Floor Space Value Added for Production
Floor Space Non-Value Added
Number of Operations to Schedule

A Guideline for Team Selection

The management person who has overall responsibility for the lean VSM event and outcome will select two team leaders—one for information flow and one for material flow. Once this is accomplished the team leaders and management will recruit team members for the VSM event.

The following is a typical guideline for selection of teams:

Material Flow	Information Flow
Operations Management	Information Technologh IT
Stores	Materials Manager
Purchasing	Supply chain Manager
Shop Associates	MRP/ERP Guru
Human Resources	Order Entry/Customer Service
Maintenance/facilities	Traffic Manager
Industrial Engineering	Sales
Purchasing	Master Scheduler
	Controller

VSM Preparation: Training, Data Collection, & Assignments

Training in the VSM Process

There are a number of one-day VSM training courses and instructors available for this event. It is wise to consider the use of a seasoned facilitator for the training and for the VSM process. You can locate resources via the Internet, NIST, or a local university offering a lean education program.

Training for our hypothetical team members at Paradise Products will consist of a six-hour workshop in Value Stream Mapping. This session prepares the team members so they understand the process, learn how to collect data, and grasp a common set of expressions and vocabulary terms.

Prior to the actual VSM process, it is essential to collect data about the business. Sub-teams in the various areas will collect this data with guidance from the program facilitator. The facilitator will ensure that the preparations are complete. Sub-teams must assemble the following data about the current business:

■ Work sample of the value stream to determine overall efficiency. At this time, knowing that a specific number of employees are assigned to the process, at pre-determined intervals the sub-team should observe the employees to determine whether they are performing value added or non-value added work. You are not attempting to determine speed or pace of employees, but to determine how badly the current process utilizes the employees assigned.

■ Inventory on hand for the value stream. (What is the value of obsolete items and the inventory category?)

■ Cost of quality for the value stream with specific attention to scrap and warranty.

■ On-time delivery to the customer for this value stream.

■ Carrying cost % for inventory.

■ Work order history: elapsed time from first operation to completion.

■ Floor Plans.

■ Organizational structure for the value stream, including all support functions.

■ Average routing set-up hours for the value stream.

■ Average hours to build one unit and historical productivity.

Current State Value Stream Maps: Material Flow Spaghetti Diagrams & Process Maps

A successful VSM event outcome requires that all team members have a good understanding of the value stream information and material required for their respective team. To ensure this each team will walk the process flows and interview people performing the work, gathering information and keeping very precise notes.

The next step is to map the process using Post-It notes to document the process.

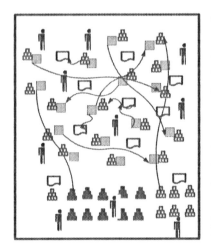

Spaghetti Diagram

A spaghetti diagram for the current material flow is completed at this time. A simple spaghetti diagram shows how much travel distance is required to complete a process. Lines are drawn on a floor plan to show movement associated with a process. These lines are then measured to calculate the total distance involved. A facility floor plan and space analysis is also posted on the team's storyboard wall (a physical location where team VSM documentation is displayed) to show how space is utilized. You are now ready to create the current state material flow value stream map.

Current State VSM: Material Flow

The current state material flow is comprised of five parts:

1. Information regarding the business: the demand for the products, the future state estimated labor required, inventory, floor space, and organization requirements for support.
2. The material flow steps.
3. Inventory days expressed in lead-time days. (This value = # of inventory units at each process step/the daily requirement for units.)
4. Specific information regarding each process step, cycle time, resources required, change over time.
5. Total labor time required to assemble/make 1 unit of product.

Material Flow-Current State Widgets

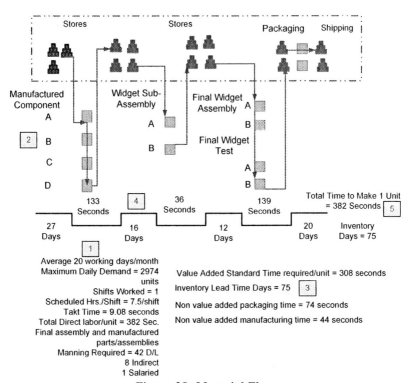

Figure 28: Material Flow

Current State Value Stream Maps: Information Flow
Current State Customer Order Process

For **Information Flow**, there are three distinct processes to map:

■ Sales & Operations Planning—the forecast.
■ Customer order management, from booking to order shipment.
■ Material replenishment, Kanban.

The current state information flow process for customer order management is mapped and non-value added (wasteful) steps are noted, in this case with a dotted line.

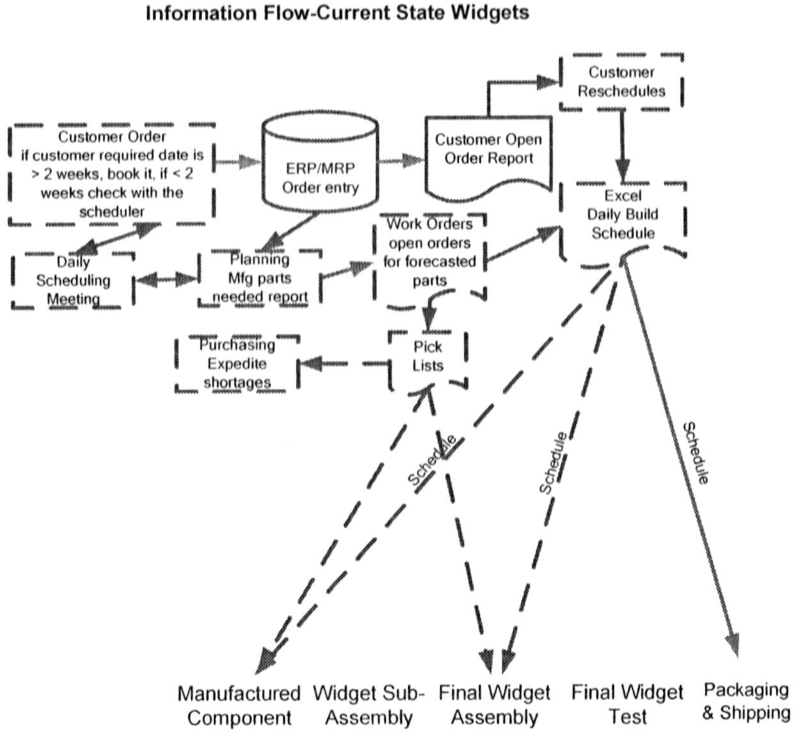

Information Flow-Current State Widgets

Figure 29: Information Flow Current State Widgets

The current state VSM shows that there are several non-value added steps in the current process, and there is a lack of accurate scheduling of customer orders at the time they are received. The future state goal is to eliminate the dotted lines—to implement a process that matches customer demand to schedule capacity and yields on-time delivery to the customer request date.

Quantify the Current State Performance Measurements

At the commencement of a sanctioned lean implementation, performance measurements were defined for improvement. These performance measurements are now quantified as a result of the current state value stream mapping process.

Performance Measurement Widgets
Quality Costs, Scrap, Warranty-Annual
On Time Delivery to Customers
Direct Labor Employees
Indirect Labor Support
Salaried Support
*Inventory Finished Goods $
* Inventory WIP $
* Inventory Raw $
Weighted Avg. Lead-Time Days Manuf.
Weighted Avg. Lead-Time Days Suppliers
Distance Traveled to Make a Product
Floor Space Value Added for Production
Floor Space Non-Value Added
Number of Operations to Schedule

Future State Value Stream Mapping
A Lean Roadmap Future State Training

At appropriate times during the VSM event, the team(s) receive training overviews that allow them to consider "out of the box" ideas for improvement. This training is useful, as many if not most of the team members have not been asked to consider Lean Roadmap alternatives to the current process, and may not understand what constitutes non-value added process steps.

During the VSM process at strategic points of discovery and future state design, short training sessions are required. The training suggested here will supplement the team knowledge, and will assist in development of the future state Lean Roadmap.

Material Flow Team: Takt time, 1-piece flow, assembly to customer order, line/cell balance, kanban

Information Flow Team: Takt time, Sales & Operations planning, supply chain management, supplier 1-line planning reports, available to promise, flattened BOMs and routings, back-flushing, lean capacity, and kanban

Both Teams: What is cost/what is waste?

The latter topic uses a sample P&L and balance sheet to demonstrate where a % of sales goes—the impact of inventory on profit. The example uses the "Seven Deadly Wastes" described next to divide the P&L and balance sheet into the wasteful areas: scrap, inventory, obsolescence, wasted floor space, warehouse costs. This discussion may well be the first time an employee has had an explanation of costs and the relationship to waste, profit, and the health of the business in the marketplace.

Identifying the "Seven Deadly Wastes"

The teams are asked to quantify current process steps and performance values as either value added, non-valued added, or required non-value added. Once this process is completed, the three categories are added up and solutions for elimination/reduction are considered as the future state Lean Roadmap processes are developed.

This brainstorming session is a pivotal activity. It is important to get the VSM team(s) to agree on a few major causes of waste (also called "undesirable effects"). The group must agree upon causes before it can agree upon specific solutions.

Non-Value added waste falls into one of seven categories:

1. **Over-Production** - Producing items that won't be shipped today. Cause: Process is not synchronized or balanced (see example below).
2. **Transportation** - Moving product around the shop to the next workstation.
3. **Correction** - Rework.
4. **Motion** - Unnecessary movement within the workstation.
5. **Waiting** - Idle workers waiting for work to be delivered to their station.
6. **Inventory** - Raw materials, work-in-progress (WIP), and finished goods.
7. **Processing** - Inefficiencies.

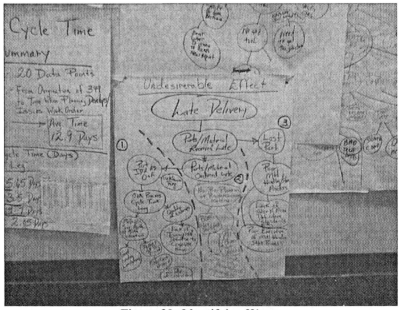

Figure 30: Identifying Waste

In addition, a number of office wastes are built into the information flow process, such as:

- Order entry not being able to schedule accurately
- Order entry checking a late shipment for a customer
- Physical inventories
- Work order opening and closing
- Inventory transactions for work in progress
- Multi-step routings with labor reported at each
- Week-old variance reports that require an explanation
- Daily scheduling meetings
- Paperwork handoffs between people and departments

Brainstorming & The Future State

At this point in the process, the team(s) are ready to brainstorm ideas for the future state process, utilizing the current state floor plans, spaghetti diagrams, process flow charts, PPQ matrix, performance measurements, and the sales forecast.

The material flow team can very easily use block floor-plan cut-outs to lay out a new material flow for the factory. Once the material flow concepts are agreed upon for either one value stream or the entire factory, the savings, costs, and timing can be developed.

The information flow team will block flowchart the sales and operations planning/supply chain process, the order management process, the shipping grid, and kanban processes. The next step will be to detail the flow in concept.

Future State Process Maps: Material Flow

The future state material flow process map is comprised of six parts:

1. Information regarding the business: the demand for the products, the future state estimated labor required, inventory, floor space, and organization requirements for support

2. The material flow steps
3. Inventory days expressed in lead-time days
4. Specific information regarding each process step, cycle time, resources required, change over time
5. Total labor required to assemble/make 1 unit of product
6. Required improvements to be completed

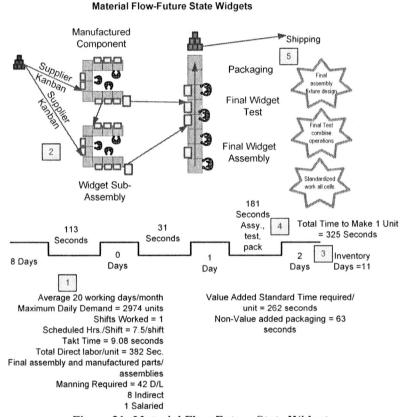

Figure 31: Material Flow Future State Widgets

Future State Process Maps: Information Flow

The Information Flow Value Stream Map is done one time for all value streams. Information flow is universal for all product families within the facility, and generally the business. This is unlike the material flow value stream maps, which are developed based on each product family geometry, bill of material, and required process steps to manufacture.

Information Flow-Future State Widgets
Order Management & Order Consolidation Grid

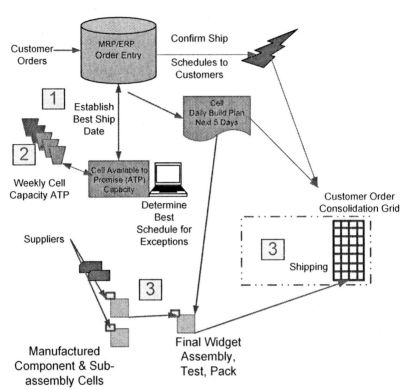

Figure 32: Order Management & Order Consolidation Grid

As customer orders are received they are scheduled using the final assembly cell for Widgets, with the best date available. This process matches customer demand to capacity, and notifies the customer service representative when the product will not ship on time.

Lean Roadmap information flow requires the definition of seven items during the future-state mapping process:

1. Sales & Operations Planning: The Forecast
2. Customer Order Management, ATC
3. Customer Order Consolidation Grid
4. Supplier 1-line Planning Report

5. Kanban, Material Replenishment
6. MRP/ERP for Lean
7. Lean Accounting

Our example for Paradise Products' electric leaf blowers shows the future state process map for customer order management. The objectives of accurately scheduling the order to a cell capacity and assigning a customer order consolidation grid were accomplished.

The Bottom Line: Calculating Savings and Presentation to Management

Upon completion of the future state value stream maps, list the major projected improvements, barriers to overcome, savings, and costs to implement. Prioritize the listing based on a logical sequential implementation and, of course, potential improvement to be gained. This list is an effective visual aid to be used in both development of the work-plan and for presentation to management, employees, and the board of directors. Here's an example:

General Areas of Presentation and Savings

Material Flow Team

- Lean Training
- Plant Layout
- Cell Layout Detail
- Assembly Cell A
    1. Set-up reduction
    2. Kanban process
    3. 5S
    4. Continuous Improvement Process
    5. Visual Factory

Information Flow Team

- Sales & Operations Planning
- Supplier 1-Line Report
- Customer Order Management, ATC
- Order Consolidation Grid
- Kanban
- ERP/MRP Configuration for Lean
- Lean Accounting

Future State Lean Roadmap Savings

Finally, determine the current cost, future state cost, savings, and cost to implement the projected changes.

Performance Measurement Widgets	Pre- Lean Roadmap Current State Value	Future State Value	Annual Savings/ income improvement
Quality Costs, Scrap, Warranty-Annual	$176,000	$50,000	$126,000
On Time Delivery to Customers	53%	95% +	
Direct Labor Employees	42	36	$180,000
Indirect Labor Support	8	4	$120,000
Salaried Support	1	1	$0
*Inventory Finished Goods $	$3,475,346	0	$139,000
* Inventory WIP $	$476,000	$42,000	$17,360
* Inventory Raw $	$1,500,456	$600,000	$36,000
Weighted Avg. Lead-Time Days Manuf.	27	2	
Weighted Avg. Lead-Time Days Suppliers	58	5	
Distance Traveled to Make a Product	6500'	1245'	
Floor Space Value Added for Production	29500 sq ft	18100	
Floor Space Non-Value Added	45000 sq ft	5400	
Number of Operations to Schedule	12	1	
		Total *	$618,360
* inventory reduction annual income computed at 4% cost of money			
Capital Cost to Implement			$78,000
Expense to Implement			$76,000

The Bottom Line

Inventory Reduction	Inventory Cost of Money at 4%	Capital Cost Required	Expense Cost Required
$4,810,000	$192,400	$78,000	$76,000
	Expense Reduction		
	$426,000		

Linking Savings and General Improvements To Lean Roadmap Building Blocks

It is advisable to link savings and improvements to specific Lean Roadmap Building Blocks. In doing so, a logical explanation to the management team, utilizing the following table, spaghetti diagrams, space utilization diagrams, and flow charts will assist in the overall explanation and discussion.

Lean Roadmap Building Block	Performance Measurement Widgets
1, 2, 11	Quality Costs, Scrap, Warranty-Annual
2, 3, 4, 5, 6, 7-9	On Time Delivery to Customers
2, 6, 8-11	Direct Labor Employees
1-11	Indirect Labor Support
1-11	Salaried Support
3, 4, 6, 7, 8, 10	*Inventory Finished Goods $
6, 10	* Inventory WIP $
7, 10	* Inventory Raw $
6, 10	Weighted Avg. Lead-Time Days Manuf.
3, 4, 7, 10	Weighted Avg. Lead-Time Days Suppliers
6	Distance Traveled to Make a Product
6	Floor Space Value Added for Production
6, 9, 10	Floor Space Non-Value Added
6	Number of Operations to Schedule
3, 5, 6	# of Operations to Schedule

2-8, 10	Make to customer order, no finished goods
6-8	Customer order scheduling at order entry, matching demand to capacity
4, 6, 7, 8, 10	On time delivery to the customer
3, 4, 7	Supplier planning coupled to business planning
3, 4, 5, 6, 10	linked to final assembly via kanban, lead-time must be reduced, and material shortages are reduced,
10	Kanban used to re-order material
6 thru 10	Reduction in supply chain lead-time
1 thru 11	Improvements in all defined performance measurements are required

Implementation Plan

The project plan is the road map for change. It includes significant detail about the scope of the project and the means of executing change.

					1st Half
ID	**0**	Task Name	Start	Finish	
1		Lean Implementation	Mon 6/9/03	Fri 4/2/04	
2	✓	Training	Mon 6/9/03	Fri 8/22/03	
9	✓	Future State Floor Plan	Wed 7/2/03	Thu 7/31/03	
14		PPQ 2 level cells	Tue 7/15/03	Mon 9/1/03	
72		Supplier 1 line planning report	Mon 8/4/03	Mon 12/29/03	
80		Sales and Operations Planning	Mon 8/18/03	Wed 9/10/03	
92		ATC, ATO & Order Consolidation Grid	Mon 7/28/03	Thu 9/25/03	
111		Assist other plant in Lean implementation	Mon 8/18/03	Thu 8/28/03	
118		PPQ 1 Cell	Mon 8/11/03	Wed 11/12/03	
165		Purchased Kanban Locations	Mon 8/25/03	Mon 12/15/03	
212					
259					

Presentation to Management

The management presentation is made by both of the Value Stream teams.

Benefits of Value Stream Mapping are:

- An internal team of employees does the work and presents the results; the report of findings is credible and has the support of the team to implement.
- Because of the short duration and focused effort, results are visible in days rather than the normal weeks of time to complete.
- Team members learn to use the basic tools of lean process design in the course of the week, making them able to conduct subsequent value stream mapping processes.
- The management and baseline team does the work and the controller keeps score.

PART IV
LEAN ROADMAP SUPPLY CHAIN MANAGEMENT:
MATERIAL FLOW DESIGN

This section will detail the Lean Roadmap design process steps for material flow, from suppliers to manufacturing to the customer, utilizing cellular manufacturing, kanban replenishment, and scheduling of final assembly cell capacity. This part of the Lean Roadmap process is much more obvious and tangible than others, such as information flow, because in material flow you can physically observe the route by which material moves through the supply chain. Lean Roadmap brings you basic design tools to simplify the design process for the material flow.

The objectives of Lean Roadmap material flow are to:

■ Reduce lead-time, beginning at receipt of a customer order, through assembly and ship, to less than the customer expectation. This is done by determining final assembly cell design requirements for each planning family cell.
■ Reduce scheduling and planning of final assembly cells by grouping the final assembly, test, and packaging into one cell; thus scheduling of one cell is required, rather than several operations.
■ Institute the storage of kanban material at final assembly cells, reordered and replenished by cell associates as consumed by the customers.
■ Design manufacturing cells that supply the final assembly cells with manufactured items.

■ Couple supply cells to final assembly cells via kanban, and couple internal supply cells to suppliers via kanban.

■ Reduce the amount of required indirect labor support by creating cells.

■ Reduce floor space required by grouping operations into cells and moving the furniture into much more compact layouts and floor-plans.

Lean Roadmap Material Flow Team & Performance Measurements

Both the team structure and performance measurements were defined during the value stream mapping process, if utilized. Otherwise, you'll need to select team members and define performance measurements prior to designing the supply chain management material flow process. During the material flow design and implementation phase, strengthening and further refinement of the team structure, membership, and performance measurements can and should be completed.

It is important to select a cross-functional team comprised of people who work in the material flow process as it is currently defined. Team members representing the following areas of the business should be considered:

■ Management Representative
■ Operations Supervision
■ Stores
■ Purchasing
■ Cell Associates
■ Human Resources
■ Maintenance Plant Controller
■ Supplier
■ Facilitator
■ Industrial Engineer

The performance measurements assist the team in staying focused on important and strategic improvements that are required for the implementation and the business to be successful. Performance measurements should include:

- Quality
- Delivery
- Cost
- Cross Training
- Safety

Material Flow Design Steps

Lean Roadmap material flow is a logical process for simplifying the design of manufacturing cells and of overall material flow through the supply chain, from supplier to customer. In this section, we define the process steps for determining cell design at maximum forecasted sales demand.

Lean Roadmap Material Flow Design

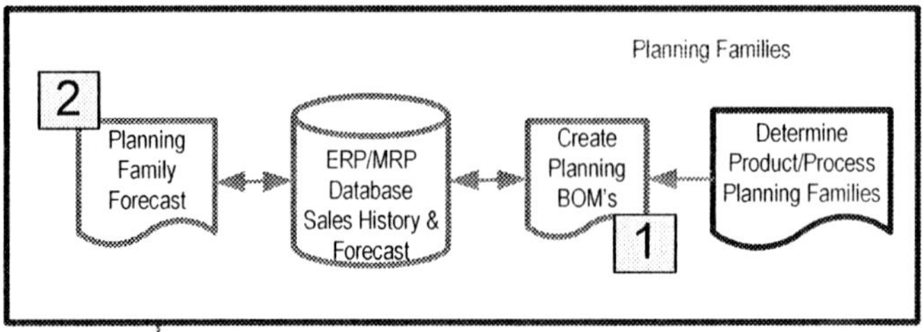

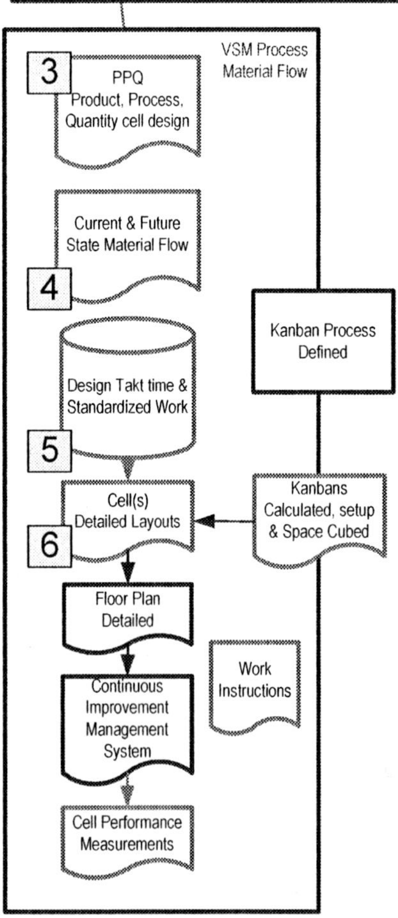

1. Create product planning family bills of material.

2. Create a planning family sales forecast.

3. Develop a 1- or 2-level PPQ matrix (product process quantity), to define current material flow.

4. Develop a current and future state overall plant material flow. (This may have already been determined in a value stream mapping event.)

5. Use the family forecast to calculate Takt time to define the cellular manufacturing process steps, stations, and manning required for maximum monthly forecasted demand.

6. Detail the cell design, considering work to be performed, assembly room required, material required, input and output stations needed for material, tooling, fixturing, work instructions, visual storyboard, material output station, and kanban station.

Figure 33: Material Flow Design

Significant improvements occur when material flow supply chain management is defined in cellular customer demand architecture:

■ Lead-time is reduced.
■ Customer on-time delivery is improved.
■ Build/assemble to customer order is made possible.
■ Kanban/material replenishment is established at the point of use, managed by the cell associates.
■ Floor space required is reduced.
■ Team/cell performance measurements are improved.
■ Scheduling complexity is reduced.

Design and implementation of a customer demand-based supply chain management architecture, wherein process steps are linked together by cell design and kanban, and managed on a daily and event basis by the people working in the process steps, is a powerful methodology that enables your business to become a leader in your served markets.

The competitor who has the shortest lead-time and a demonstrated history of on-time delivery to the customer's request date commands an opportunity to price at a somewhat higher level than the competition. (Your sales force will support selective pricing increases given shortened lead-time.) A lean internal supply-chain structure that eliminates finished goods inventory and implements customer-demand cellular material flow will free up 25% to 60% of the company's floor space; you now can utilize the same bricks and mortar to add additional product lines, acquisitions, or customer integrated processes with little to no additional overhead increase.

Notes:
1. **Please, take the time to include others in the design process. Utilize a stepped and logical design process, and obtain accurate data to design the material flow and cell layout.**
2. **Do not attempt to implement cells where the process yields poor quality and/or is not predictable. With a poor yield process, when the furniture is pushed**

**together and the inventory drained, the options to
move people to work on another item/order is
removed, and the situation can actually be made
worse.**

**It is important to review Part III of this book on
value stream mapping (VSM). Part III explains how
to develop planning family bills of material and the
two-level PPQ (product process quantity), which
simplifies the conceptual design of manufacturing
cells required for efficient material flow.**

Building Block 3: Product Planning Families

A planning family bill of material (BOM) is created for each
product sales planning family. This Planning BOM resides on
your current MRP/ERP processor and is used to create a
forecast, using sales history and market intelligence. The
forecast is then used to plan the design of manufacturing cells
for maximum expected monthly sales demand and efficient
factory layout.

Post-lean cellular implementation will require Product
Planning Families as an integral part of the sales and operations
planning process detailed in Part III.

Bills of material are listings of material required to make a
product, and in the order of manufacture, planning bills are
simply a listing of all saleable-product configurations for the
planning family. A single-level planning bill residing on your
MRP/ERP database would look like this:

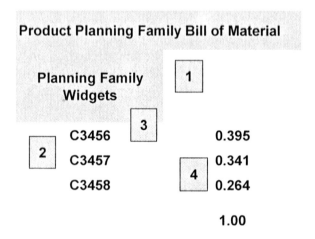

Figure 34: Bill of Material

1. A product planning family bill of material number should be the family name description for ease of company discussions, such as Widgets.
2. The product planning family model number (Widgets) is the parent number, and the top level in the bill of material. All product models sold/planned in the family are at Level 1 child, and are linked directly to the parent number.
3. The planning family part/model numbers are the actual part numbers assigned to the products that are sold as members of the family, and are your catalogue numbers for each configuration.

The quantity per bill of material for each member of the family is the forecasted % **planned** for each product (modified to reflect any market intelligence). For example, a total of 100 units of product for the Widget product planning family are forecasted for sales planning. 39 of the units are planned for C3456, which is 39% of the total planning family forecast.

Building Block 4: Product Planning Family Sales Forecast

The sales forecast for the family is determined by simply entering one forecasted quantity of units for each family and for each calendar month. The number of units times the planning family % in the BOM yields the correct quantity to plan for each family member. In the following illustration,

1. The product planning family quantity planned for May 2004 is 54732 units.
2. The historical experience for C3456 as a part of the family is 39.5%. Therefore we are forecasting 21616 units for C3456.

		Forecast					
		May-04	Jun-04	Jul-04	Aug-04	Total	
Planning Family Widgets		20	25	19	20	84	Average/ day forecasted
C3456	2	21616	27021	20536	21616	90789	1081
C3457		18683	23354	17749	18683	78470	934
C3458		14432	18040	13711	14432	60615	722
Sales Forecast	1	54732	68415	51995	54732	229874	2737
Average Units/Day		2737	2737	2737	2737	2737	

Figure 35: Sales Forecast Chart

Building Block 5: PPQ—Product, Process, Quantity Cell & Plant Layout

PPQ, product process quantity, is a weighted average calculation used to determine the resources required to meet a forecast of families of product. This information is used for cell design and factory layout in the future state. The process yields information required to develop a material flow in hours/days as opposed to weeks/months.

PPQ Level 1 is a graphic table of the final assembly, including test resources required for final assembly of products. PPQ Level 2 is a graphic table of the manufacturing resources required to design manufacturing cells that will supply the final assembly cells as defined in PPQ Level 1.

PPQ Level 1—Final Assembly Cells

The PPQ uses either historical sales or preferably forecasted sales in units by planning family and part/assembly routing standard operation times for the current process, and calculates the hours required at each work center/resource required for the manufacture of the products at both PPQ Levels 1 & 2.

Widget Final Assembly, Test & Package Cell

PPQ Level 1 Final Assembly Routing Sequence and Standard Cycle Time

1 Operation Work Ctrs	Step 1	Step 2	Step 3	Step 4	Step 5	Step 6	Total
Planning Family Widgets Set Up Hrs.	0.00	0.00 **2**	0.00	0.00	0.00	0.00	0.00
C3456 Cycle Times	30	27	29	26	31	27	170
C3457 Seconds	31	29	32	27	36	29	184
C3458	33	32	36	29	39	32	201
Weighted Avg Times	31	29	32	27 **3**	35	29	183
Forecasted Takt Time Seconds	9.87	9.87	9.87	9.87	9.87 **5**	9.87 **4**	
Stations Required	3.2	2.9	3.2	2.8	3.5	2.9	18.5

Figure 36: Final Assembly Chart

The Level 1 PPQ calculation reveals the following information:

1. The routing work centers required for all top-level assemblies required for the Product planning Families within the family.

2. The routing standard times for each final assembly step in the planning family routings, for all products in the planning family.
3. The weighted average cycle time for the family, derived from the weighted average of the family member quantity required for the period times the standard time, divided by the total family quantity forecasted. Please note that 35 is highlighted. This is the process constraint and is used to determine the cell capacity for use in ATC.
4. The forecasted Takt time based on the current level of hours worked per day and the machine/process effectiveness.
5. The number of stations required is adjusted to meet the Takt time. In this case six operation steps (routing steps) have been identified, with a manning/station requirement of 18.5.

PPQ Level 1 Takt Time

Takt Time is the rate at which the process must produce product to meet customer demand. Takt time is expressed as the cycle time that product must be produced within a final assembly cell to meet customer demand. The calculation for Takt time is available daily *effective* scheduled hours of work/the total units required for the day.

Takt time calculations are utilized twice in Lean Roadmap, once for cell design at maximum monthly sales forecast, and daily to plan for cell resources required.

1. Takt time is used in the design of the process, taking the maximum monthly forecasted demand for the products to be produced in the final assembly cell and utilizing the weighted average total standard time for the final assembly or production cell.
2. Takt time is used on a daily basis to determine the build/assembly cycle frequency to meet customer demand and, from the Takt time calculation and a standardized work sheet (covered later), to determine the

manning requirement and work assignment for the final assembly cell.

The design Takt time calculation is used to rough-cut the number of stations/positions required to match capacity to maximum forecasted customer demand. The Takt time calculations for line design of stations required are:

1. The weighted average cycle/total standard time from PPQ Level 1.
2. The Cell/Line design Takt time = effective scheduling time/shift times the number of shifts worked/day divided by the number of units of product required/forecasted per day..
3. The stations required is simply the total weighted average cycle time divided by the Takt time, to yield 18.5 stations.

Widget Final Assembly Cell, Takt Time and Stations/Manning

Line/Process Name: <u>Product Planning</u> Family Widgets

From Standard Work Combination Chart or Production Capacity Sheet

Weighted average total Cycle Time ___ | 1 | 182.95

all calculations must be in the same units of measure

Process Design Takt Time = (Effective working Time/shift X # of shifts)

| 2 | The Daily Production units required

___ seconds/shift   # of shifts

$$\frac{27000}{2,737} \quad \begin{array}{c} X \\ = \end{array} \quad \frac{1}{9.87}$$

Units/day required   Takt Time

Number of Stations Required = weighted Average Total Cycle / Total Std. Time

weighted Average | 3 |
Total Cycle / Std Time

$$\frac{182.95}{9.87} \quad = \quad \frac{\text{\# of Stations}}{18.54}$$

Process Design Takt
Time

Figure 37: PPQ 1 Work Combination Chart

PPQ Level 2   Internal Manufacturing Supplier Cells

A Level 2 PPQ defines the manufacturing resources required by each planning family to design cells that support the final assembly cells with manufactured parts and assemblies required to assemble the product family products. It is well worth noting that PPQ 2 cells very often supply multiple PPQ1 final assembly cells.

The following illustration represents work centers that supply product to a final assembly PPQ 1 cell.

Widget Sub Assembly Cell

PPQ Level 2 Internal Supplier Routing Sequence and Standard Cycle Time

	Operation Work Ctrs	Step 1	Step 2	Step 3	Step 4	Step 5	Step 6	Total
1								
Planning Family Widgets	Set Up Hrs.	0.20	0.15	0.09	0.00	0.00	0.00	0.44
2342	Cycle Times	40	42	26	15	14	15	152
2345	2 Seconds	37	32	31	17	15	17	149
2365		27	32	29	20	17	14	139
3	Weighted Avg Times	36	36	28	17	15	15	148
	Forecasted Takt Time	9.866	9.866	9.866	9.866	9.866	9.866	4
5	Stations Required	3.603	3.644	2.888	1.7232	1.534	1.563	14.955

Figure 38: PPQ Level 2 Chart

The PPQ Level 2 defines the work centers required to supply all manufactured items required for the assembly cells for the planning family items sold to customers. With the PPQ Level 1 and 2 defined, a current state conceptual material flow can be developed.

Utilizing the PPQ, a current state material flow can be developed. Using the PPQ routings and floor plans, it is a fairly straightforward exercise to map the material flow. The PPQ gives us routing times, which may be adjusted based on demonstrated ratios of efficiency/performance to standard.

Notes:
1. **All product planning families should be processed through the PPQ calculation. Once processed, then sort by importance to the business, such as by descending $ in sales, $ profit, or some other important measure. We want to design cells starting with the highest priority measure of importance first.**
2. **A Level 2 PPQ internal supplier cell is not scheduled at order entry using the Available to Capacity logic. Manning for the supplier cells is determined at Sales & Operations Planning (S&OP), and is adjusted as**

required using an internal supplier-cell schedule board. ATC prevents the over-scheduling of final assembly cells. This process also minimizes any over-scheduling of internal supplier cells.

3. A PPQ is not required for very simple manufacturing processes—those with few products and steps in a family. Additionally, when a business does not have routings and standard times residing in digital format, then use the standardized work tools.

Current State Material Flow
Planning Family Widgets

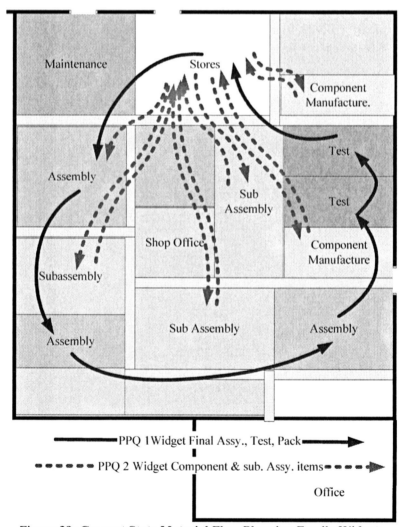

Figure 39: Current State Material Flow Planning Family Widgets

The current state material flow (spaghetti diagram) and value stream map reveals the level of waste in the current material movement process. The goal is to utilize the current state material flow, the PPQ, the VSM non-value added steps, and the material flow team knowledge to design a future state material flow in block diagram.

Building Block 6: Future State Conceptual Material Flow Cellular Layout Floor Plan Design

The future state conceptual material flow is developed utilizing the current state flow and the PPQ for Levels 1 and 2. The goal is to couple the process steps together and enable 1-piece mixed model flow from operation to operation.

Future State Material Flow
Planning Family Widgets

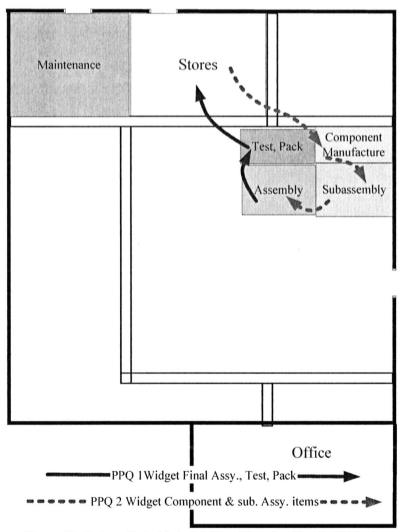

Figure 40: Future State Material Flow Planning Family Widgets

This process also requires knowledge of the equipment available for all families of products, the need for batch processes within the 1-piece flow process, such as heat treat, and where to position strategic material point-of-use kanbans.

The future state flow product family A shows that the Level 2 PPQ has the process steps linked and in a cell, and that cell linked to the Level 1 PPQ equipment, which has also been positioned into a cell. Kanban racks have also been positioned at the cell. We now have conceptual flows, Takt time calculations, equipment lists, products that are to be processed in the cells, and a Lean Roadmap team. The next step in the process is to complete the VSM savings chart (savings, cost, time to implement), present the findings to management, get the approvals, notify the people affected, and commence with the next steps.

Notes:
1. **Several planning family members are likely to utilize the same work center numbers.**
2. **Where there are multiple work centers for the same process step, break them up and position them in the appropriate block cells, keeping in mind the PPQ capacity required.**

Concepts in Cellular Material Flow (1-Piece Mixed Model Flow)

The concept of one-piece flow is to move one piece at a time through the linked process steps. As the process steps are linked, you will need to balance the station cycle times within the cell to allow for one-piece flow. This is accomplished using the standardized work process (discussed later), combined with a teamwork mentality among cell associates, a willingness to share work of others adjacent to them to effectively balance the operation cycle times within the cell.

One-piece flow has several advantages:

- Lead-time is reduced.
- Customer orders are assembled as received.
- The space required is reduced.
- The exposure to production of defective products is reduced.
- The one-piece-per-station exposes imbalance in the process.
- Teamwork and sharing of the workload is enhanced.

One Piece Mixed Model Flow
Small: Parts and Assemblies

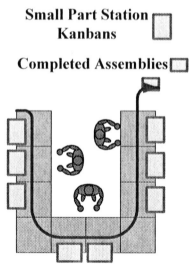

Figure 41: One Piece Mixed Model Flow – Small Parts

The difficulties associated with one-piece flow design and implementation are to balance the operations that are coupled and to demonstrate to employees that doing one step at a time is as efficient as doing a batch of product at any one time. It is advisable to use one of the cell simulation exercises that are commercially available to demonstrate the overall advantages that one-piece flow has over batch manufacturing.

Cell Design Concepts: U and Line

There are several configurations in cell design for assembly and machine tool cells. The primary design configurations for assembly are the basic U shape and the straight-line design. I will limit my discussion to these two basic designs and the reasons for selecting one versus the other.

The U cell is used for products that feature small cube-size parts, small assembly size, and short-cycle-time. The product to be assembled must be easily conveyed from station to station. The primary advantage of the U cell is the ability to change the team size based on Takt time, and still have a short walking distance from station to station within the cell. Kanbans are easily replenished, and are located within easy reach to operators. As the Takt time changes, so do the cell manning and the range of assembly stations/operations for each operator.

The linear assembly cell is used for physically large cube-size products, where product size becomes too large to manage in a U cell, such as automobile assembly. In line design, small parts are stored at the station where space permits, and large parts may be stored behind the operator. This allows operators to freely move from station to station when manning is varied to meet Takt time changes. In a line design, the walking distance is generally great from Station 1 to the final assembly operation. The cell may be designed in such a way that with varying Takt times, the line may operate fully staffed for a varying amount of time to accommodate changing demand, as opposed to the U design, where either the manning level or hours of operation is adjusted.

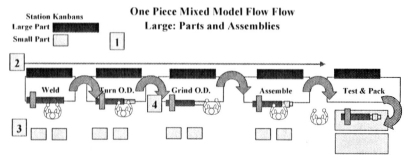

Figure 42: One Piece Mixed Model Flow - Large Parts

Standardized Work

Upon completion of the future-state material-flow block diagram, performance measurement justification, and overall management buy-in, the next step in the process is to select a planning family or group of product planning families that utilize the same process steps and equipment, and define the cell process steps and stations required to meet maximum monthly forecasted demand for the products.

We have already completed a PPQ Levels 1 & 2. We have the equipment required, the stations required, and the required Takt time. The cell design can be easily accomplished utilizing a process know as standardized work.

Standardized work is a process that identifies all operational steps that will be included in the cell, assigns an average time for each element, identifies value and non-value added for future improvement, and provides information required to vary manning assignments within the cell at varying customer demand levels. In cellular 1-piece flows manufacturing, standardized work is required to properly staff cells to meet varying customer demand, while maintaining consistent methodology in the manufacture of the products.

Standardized Work steps are:

1. Identify the product planning families to be studied.
2. Ensure that process quality yield and process reliability are ready for 1-piece flow.

3. Notify employees; seek buy-in and participation.
4. Provide basic standardized work training to employees affected.
5. Create a list of all parts consumed in the cells, and calculate kanban levels for the cell.
6. Complete a production capacity sheet. (This sheet is used for high volume production and is illustrated later.)
7. Complete a standardized work sheet (illustrated later).

■ **Note: At this time identify items that are non-value added, and make a list of Continuous Improvement items to be addressed.**

■ **Make sure you are sufficiently detailed in identifying and recording the work elements; this is vital to proper balancing of the cell at varying cycle times.**

8. Complete a work assignment graphic for varying Takt times.
9. Determine what point-of-use materials are to be stored at each location. As you observe the assembly operations, record the point-of-use material consumed at each process step.
10. Count out and containerize point-of-use kanbans for each station. This will demonstrate the physical cube size required.
11. Determine the space required at the station to build/assemble one unit.
12. Identify tooling required at each station and where it will be stored.
13. Identify all fixturing required and where it will be stored.
14. Identify the material output area, and input area as required for the cell.
15. Implement the cell floor plan, and be prepared to work with the cell associates over time to solve problems and fine tune the running of the cell. **Note: Use the 5S process described later to tag and eliminate all items not required in the cell. Do not move non-required items into the cell.**
16. Verify that Takt time can be met as calculated, and that the cell cycle time is balanced between cell stations.

17. Develop pictorial work instruction guides, and get feedback from cell associates.
18. Implement a visual storyboard for performance measurements, delivery, quality, productivity, non-value added, and safety.
19. Implement a cell-led Continuous Improvement process.

Benefits derived from standardized work are:

- Reduction in variation
- One-piece flow design
- Workstation organization
- Line balance
- Lead-time reduction
- Team performance measurements
- Ergonomic improvements
- Simplified scheduling
- Simple manning assignments with varying Takt time
- Improved on-time delivery

Production Capacity Sheet

The production capacity sheet is a valuable tool for:

- Determining all of the work elements, both current state and after the future-state cell is in place
- Determining the time required for each work element
- Determining and comparing the capacity per day to the forecasted demand per day.

This makes it a valuable tool for cell design.

PPQ 1 Product Planning Family Widgets, Final Assy. [5]	Production Capacity Sheet	[1] Time Units minutes			PF&D 5%		Takt Time [2] 9.87		Daily Demand 2737 [3]	Scheduling Time/Day 27000 [4]	Capacity/Day 2737 [15] [13]		
Work Center	Operation Element Description	[6] 2 3 4 [7] 5 6 7 8 9 10							Total Elapsed Element Time [8]	# Of Units built [9]	Average Elemental Time [10]	Takt Time [11]	Stations required
Step 1		31.00 32.00 33.00 30.00 29.00 28.00 33.00 37.00 28.00 29.0							310.00	10.00	10.00	31	3.1
Step 2		29.00 31.00 28.00 27.00 32.00 33.00 29.00 28.00 27.00 28.00							292.00	10.00	29	9.87	3.0
Step 3		31.00 34.00 30.00 33.00 30.00 29.00 33.00 33.00 31.00 31.00							315.00	10.00	32	9.87	3.2
Step 4		27.00 26.00 28.00 25.00 27.00 29.00 28.00 26.00 28.00 29.00							273.00	10.00	27	9.87	2.8
Step 5		38.00 33.00 35.00 36.00 34.00 37.00 32.00 33.00 37.00 36.00							351.00	10.00 [12]	35	9.87	3.6
Step 6		29.00 30.00 28.00 29.00 32.00 30.00 32.00 27.00 28.00 29.00							294.00	10.00	29	9.87	3.0
	Send to Stores											9.87	0.0
	Time for 1 Cycle:	185 186 182 180 184 186 187 184 179 182							Total	183.50 [14]			18.6
									PPQ 1	28.80			

Figure 43: Production Capacity Sheet

To create a Production Capacity sheet, first determine the time units you will use. In this example we are using minutes. When we previously completed the PPQ Level 1, we used standard hours from the routing files. The above illustration steps.

1. The time units used.
2. The Takt time at forecast.
3. The daily demand at forecast.
4. The available scheduling time per day. **Note: Be careful to use demonstrated time available** and not what we all wish it were.
5. The current work center/station within the cell.
6. The elemental detail of the work, waiting, and walking time observed. In the example, there is not a lot of detail. But when you do your observations, be detailed. This will be helpful in balancing work between cell stations.
7. In the example, ten observations were taken for each element. As a rule of thumb, the higher the volume and/or shorter the total cycle time, the more observations you should take. For instance, assembling laptop computers would be a relatively short total cycle time, while assembling an air conditioning condenser

for a 40-story building would not. But the laptop requires a finer detail of station balance than the condenser. For the condenser, while elemental detail is important for station design, the concept of a team, with assembly associates assisting one another to better smooth the cell imbalance, is most important. **Note: During the observation phase, make a list of the tools and fixtures used at each station, and a list of the direct materials required at each operation. (Use the bills of material and ensure accuracy of actual build to the engineering bills of material BOMs.)**

8. The elapsed time, i.e., the summation of the observation clock time taken for this element of work.
9. The total number of units built for the observations taken.
10. The average elemental time = total elapsed time/# of units produced.
11. The Takt time required for each element.
12. Any bottleneck constraint elements; in this example, step 5
13. The number of cell stations required for each work element = average elemental time divided by the Takt time.
14. The total number of stations required.
15. The daily cell capacity as defined by hours worked.

Combination Sheet

The combination sheet is used to define station-manning assignment at varying Takt times, and is the basis for cell station design. This sheet is used for two purposes: cell design and fine-tuning after the cell is in place, and to update the cell assignments, layout, etc., over time as improvements are made and as product changes evolve.

The example below shows how to use the sheet for cell design. The numbered elements are:

Sta No.	Work Center	Operation Element Description	Average Elemental Time	Cumulative Time	Takt Time	Stations required
1	Step 1		31.00	31.00	9.87	3.14
	Step 2		29.20	60.20	9.87	2.96
	Step 3		31.50	91.70	9.87	3.19
	Step 4		27.30	119.00	9.87	2.77
	Step 5		35.10	154.10	9.87	3.56
	Step 6		29.40	183.50	9.87	2.98
	Time for 1 Cycle		183.50			18.60
	PPQ 1		28.80			

Figure 44: Combination Sheet

1. The work center, which is the same one as used on the Production Capacity sheet.
2. The work elements.
3. The average elemental time from the production capacity sheet.
4. The cumulative element time, used to balance work between cell stations.
5. A comparison of observed time for 1 cycle, and the original PPQ1. Do not be surprised if these two numbers are not close by comparison.
6. The number of stations required to meet forecasted Takt time.
7. The number of stations/associates required .
8. Each vertical line is placed at one element of Takt time times the number of stations required for that element. You will notice that the elapsed time in each period of Takt time is fairly well balanced in time per station. This balancing of work elements allows for a smooth flow of product within the cell from station to station.

Standardized Work Assignment Sheet

The standardized work assignment sheet is a graphic presentation of primary manning assignments at specific manning levels.

Widget Final Assembly
Standardized Work Assignment Sheet at a Takt Time of 9.87 Seconds

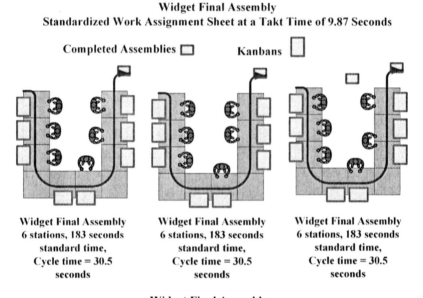

Completed Assemblies ☐   Kanbans ☐

Widget Final Assembly	Widget Final Assembly	Widget Final Assembly
6 stations, 183 seconds	6 stations, 183 seconds	6 stations, 183 seconds
standard time,	standard time,	standard time,
Cycle time = 30.5	Cycle time = 30.5	Cycle time = 30.5
seconds	seconds	seconds

Widget Final Assembly
3 cells will equate to an aggregate Takt Time of 30.5 seconds/3 = 10.1 seconds. The forecasted Takt time of 9.87 seconds is achieved with more hours worked, or process improvements.
Figure 45: Final Widget Assembly

In the illustration shown, with a Takt time of 9.87, a total of 18 stations/operators are required. The standardized work assignment sheet shows manning and stations/steps performed by each cell associate, as required to meet the forecasted Takt time.

There are a number of varying cell designs to be considered for the Widget product, the one illustrated gives us flexibility in two important ways.

1. Each cell contains all six of the final assembly steps required to assemble, test and package the Widgets, therefore, each cell can run independently to accommodate varying Takt times.
2. A cell can also be operated with from 1 to 6 people to accommodate further fluctuations in Takt time.

Kanban: Material Storage at the Point of Use

From the production capacity sheet, combination sheet, and the bills of material matrix, we now have identified which direct materials are to be used at each station. Next, determine the amount of material to be stored at each station. The quantity may be a kanban quantity if this is the only consumption point for the material, and the physical size of the kanban can be accommodated at the point of use. Most likely, the cell material locations will hold a fixed quantity of product that fits into the cell station. This quantity will be replaced as a fixed quantity of material from a kanban location.

Establish the quantity to be stored in the cell location, set up the kanbans, and determine how best to locate the items in the cell.

Kanban quantity space required at the cell to build all
models of a product planning family.

Figure 46: Identify Space Required – Photo 1

Determine the area required to perform the value added work
required to make/assemble one unit of product. The area
should be compact and allow space to work safely.

Figure 47: Identify Space Required – Photo 2

Fixtures and Tooling

Identify tooling required to perform the work required and determine where the tooling will be located for ease of use. Tooling can be placed on balancers, located on a bench, arranged along the side of a bench, or be connected to a machine tool. As always, safety and ergonomic design is important.

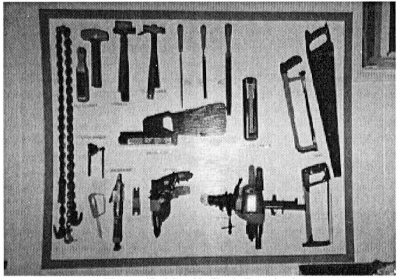

Figure 48: Identify Tools Required

Cell Implementation: 5S Work Place Organization

5S is an effective five-step process for developing and maintaining workplace organization. I strongly suggest you use this process to eliminate those items that have accumulated over the years and are not required in the cell. Do this prior to moving the furniture into position. Over the years, I have merged several U.S. businesses into fewer U.S. locations. After all of the required equipment and materials have been removed and transferred to the new location, the manufacturing floors in the closed locations were covered with items not required to operate the business.

A cell that is organized creates a real sense of pride and ownership for the people working in the cell and is also impressive to customers. Workplace organization and good housekeeping imply high quality. Several 5S videos and formal training materials are commercially available.

The 5S steps are:

1. **Sort.** Remove any item not required to produce product. This also applies to excess inventory located in the cell. The steps to follow are:
   a. Red-tag all unneeded items
   b. Sort these items out and remove them
2. **Set in Order.** A place for everything required and everything in its place. Information and steps required are:
   a. Equipment/furniture floor plan
   b. Station design
   c. Tool boards
   d. Material handling
   e. Kanban storage
   f. Floor and bench/station labels and outlines for material
   g. Move the furniture into place.
3. **Shine.** Clean all items in the cell. Polish, paint, and sharpen items as required. Steps to follow are:
   a. Clean the equipment.
   b. Clean the floors.
   c. Provide proper lighting.
   d. Label items such as kanban part numbers. These can be temporary until the cell is in place.
4. **Standardize.** Establish a list of standards for the cell concerning paint colors, labeling, frequency of applying 5S steps to the cell—daily, weekly, monthly. Steps to follow:
   a. Paint.
   b. Label.

    c. Create a standardization check-off list for maintaining the area.
5. **Sustain.** Maintain the cell, keeping the 5S achievements in place.

Generally, once 5S is completed and the physical cell configuration is in place, the people working in the cell demonstrate pride in their accomplishment and are willing to work at keeping it clean and organized. The area stands out in the factory from the rest of the facility, and employees in the other areas are quick to ask that the 5S process be used in their areas.

Takt Time Verification

When the cell is in place, work with the cell associates to:

1. Verify that cell design Takt time can be achieved.
2. Make a list of items that need to be improved upon. For those items that can be addressed quickly, do them now.

Work Instruction Guides (WIGs)

While working with the cell associates, develop work instruction guides for each position in the cell. The work instruction guides should:

1. Be as generic as possible to cover all planning family members with one guide per family. This is accomplished by referring to the engineering drawing and BOM for part identification.
2. Use pictures and a minimal requirement for verbiage.
3. Verify the usefulness of the WIGs by having the cell associates use them in actual production of the product.

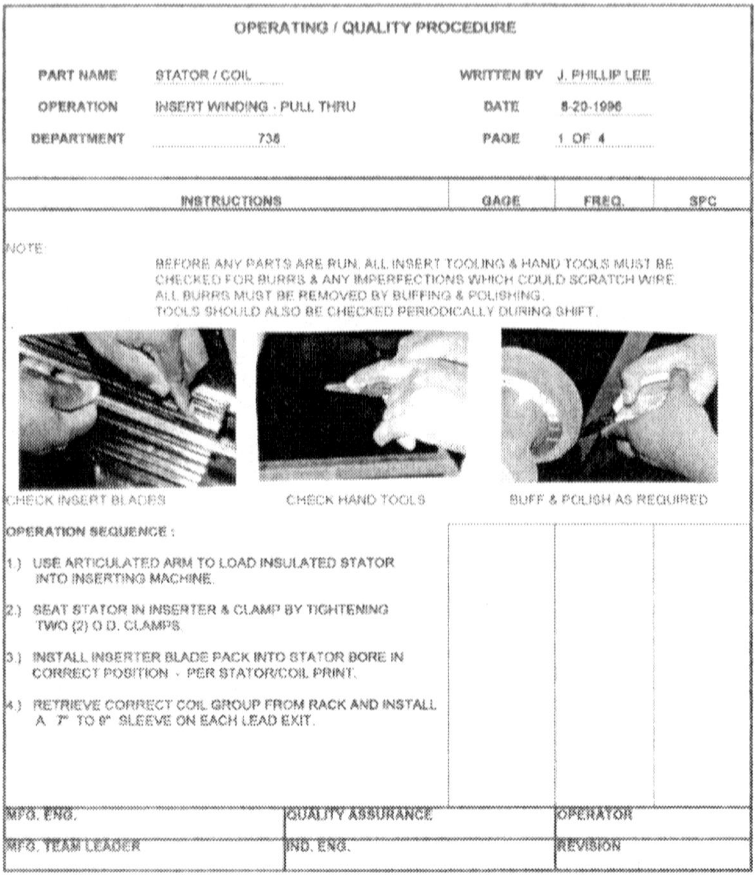

OPERATING / QUALITY PROCEDURE

PART NAME STATOR / COIL
WRITTEN BY J. PHILLIP LEE
OPERATION INSERT WINDING - PULL THRU
DATE 8-20-1996
DEPARTMENT 738
PAGE 1 OF 4

INSTRUCTIONS	GAGE	FREQ.	SPC

NOTE:
BEFORE ANY PARTS ARE RUN, ALL INSERT TOOLING & HAND TOOLS MUST BE CHECKED FOR BURRS & ANY IMPERFECTIONS WHICH COULD SCRATCH WIRE.
ALL BURRS MUST BE REMOVED BY BUFFING & POLISHING.
TOOLS SHOULD ALSO BE CHECKED PERIODICALLY DURING SHIFT.

CHECK INSERT BLADES
CHECK HAND TOOLS
BUFF & POLISH AS REQUIRED

OPERATION SEQUENCE :

1.) USE ARTICULATED ARM TO LOAD INSULATED STATOR INTO INSERTING MACHINE.

2.) SEAT STATOR IN INSERTER & CLAMP BY TIGHTENING TWO (2) O.D. CLAMPS.

3.) INSTALL INSERTER BLADE PACK INTO STATOR BORE IN CORRECT POSITION - PER STATOR/COIL PRINT.

4.) RETRIEVE CORRECT COIL GROUP FROM RACK AND INSTALL A 7" TO 8" SLEEVE ON EACH LEAD EXIT.

MFG. ENG.	QUALITY ASSURANCE	OPERATOR
MFG. TEAM LEADER	IND. ENG.	REVISION

Figure 49: Work Instruction Guides

Visual Storyboard

Prior to installing a cell visual storyboard with performance measurements, there are three items to address:

1. Include members of the cell in the discussion regarding the need for a storyboard, the contents, and maintenance of the board.
2. Design and implement a continuous improvement process for the cell that focuses on identification and elimination of waste. Emphasize that performance

measurements are measurements of management for the most part, and not cell associates.

3. Determine which performance measurements are important, how they will be calculated and by whom, and how displayed.

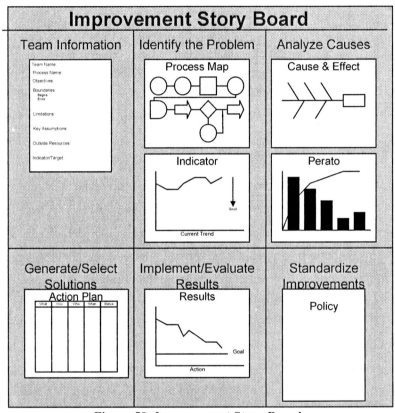

Figure 50: Improvement Story Board

The performance measurements should be standardized for the factory, based on:

■ Quality. A very high first-pass yield to design and customers' specifications is required. Without quality products, customers will leave.

■ Delivery. On-time delivery to ATC from the cell, and on-time delivery to the customer ask/promise date at shipping,

■ Cost/productivity, earned hours to paid hours. Do not focus on productivity, focus on elimination of non-value added in the cell, and productivity will take care of itself,

■ Other performance measurements are Health/safety and cross training.

PART V SUPPLY CHAIN MANAGEMENT
LEAN ROADMAP INFORMATION FLOW DESIGN

Lean Roadmap Information Flow is the heart and soul of a successful just-in-time supply chain management system. But ironically, the ability to control and process the information required to manage a lean supply chain is the least known and understood of all the elements of just-in-time lean manufacturing.

Accurate, timely information is vital for:

1. Supply chain **planning** levels for direct material and capacity from supplier and through manufacturing and distribution.
2. Ongoing daily supply chain **management** of the supply chain, matching capacity to customer demand, and replacing materials throughout the supply chain as the customers consume them.

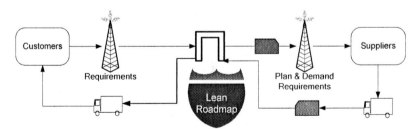

Figure 51: Information Flow Design

Lean Roadmap information flow enables the business goals of elimination/significant reduction of finished goods inventory and improvement in on-time delivery to customers. The lack of a fundamental information process as part of the lean implementation results in incremental gains, but does not address the quantum gains that are achievable, such as elimination of finished goods inventory, warehouse space, equipment, and excess employee resources.

Lean Roadmap information flow is built around three primary information processes

1. Sales and Operations Planning -- Establishing the supply chain capacity and materials required
2. Available to Capacity (ATC) -- Matching final product assembly cellular capacity to customer demand on a variable basis as dictated by the customers
3. Kanban -- Replenishment of materials as consumed by the customers.

The development of *material flow* through the factory utilizing manufacturing cells and kanban material replenishment is well known and understand in lean implementation. For the most part manufacturers have been successfully implementing production cells for decades. But the organization and management of information in the supply chain is less obvious and often escapes us. It is this facet of lean that makes for a successful and dramatically profitable implementation.

Poor information flow in, out, and around the MRP/ERP business software creates a tremendous need for excessive overhead to manage the daily chaos present in a conventional MRP/ERP process flow. Lean Roadmap defines what you must do to utilize your current business software and easily configure it into a weapon in your competitive supply-chain arsenal.

Consider the following. Let's say the actual elapsed clock time required to assemble, test, and package one of your products is 15 minutes. The customer wants the product shipped today. Is there any reason why you cannot eliminate finished goods inventory, assemble the unit ordered, and ship it today? The answer is likely no. The reasons for not doing so will be due to lack of information planning and management, and not cellular operation. To drive the point home, verify this for yourself, with one of your products: actual touch time (hands-on assembly, test, and packaging time) as compared to the actual elapsed time from the first element of work on the product to the last.

Lean Roadmap addresses the information flow required for design, planning, and management of the supply chain. New, yet proven Lean Roadmap information flow components allow for conversion of your current business software investment to complement operating in a lean environment with a minimum of overhead support.

Lean Roadmap Information Flow Chart

Lean Roadmap Information Flow

1. Develop a Sales & Operations process, which is performed at least monthly for the purposes of planning the supply chain levels for direct material and capacity.

2. Notify supplier when demand changes using a supplier 1 line per item planning report.

3. The capacity for each final assembly cell, expressed as units/ week based on a weighted average mix, and demonstrated throughput, is utilized in the available to capacity ATC software at customer order entry. This use of cell capacity at order entry prevents unknowingly over booking cell capacity in any week.

4. All customer orders are assigned a consolidation grid number as a collection for that order. The final assembly cells build to the ATC schedule and the items are consolidated at a specific floor location for shipment.

5. When S&OP is re-calculated, all kanbans are also re-calculated, and only those that vary more than a given % are acted upon.

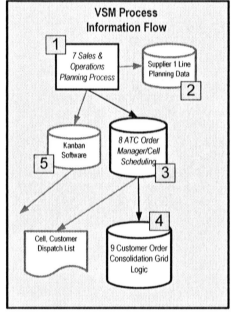

Figure 52: Information Flow Chart

The first information process in the Lean Roadmap is sales and operations planning. This process is a very effective yet easy way to establish the supply chain plan, and levels of material and capacity required to meet the sales forecast. Kanbans are recalculated at this time and those requiring a change are acted upon.

7 Sales & Operations Planning

1 Sales & Operations Planning used to adjust the capacity and material in the supply chain

2 Manufacturing kanban levels are adjusted to meet the Sales Plan

3 Final Assembly Cell staffing levels are determined and made available

4 The supplier 1 line per item planning report is updated and sent to the supplier who then adjusts their supply chain material and capacity levels.

5 The available to capacity per week for each final assembly cell is updated with a new capacity per week in units.

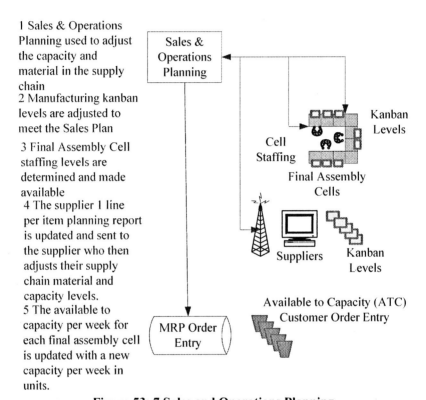

Figure 53: 7 Sales and Operations Planning

Available to Capacity (ATC) is a process developed by Bottom Line Consultants, Inc. and is the key process for matching final product assembly cell capacity to customer demand at the time of customer order receipt. This is a tremendously powerful process, yet very easy to implement. Essentially customer demand is matched to capacity in weekly buckets of time. When a customer order line item exceeds the customer want date, the master scheduler is alerted and action is taken to meet the date and satisfy the customer.

The customer build plan is available at each final assembly cell and is sorted by due date and then item type. The customer build plan also supplies a Takt time for the final assembly cell, which is used to plan manning for that day or week of assembly.

8 Available to Capacity (ATC)

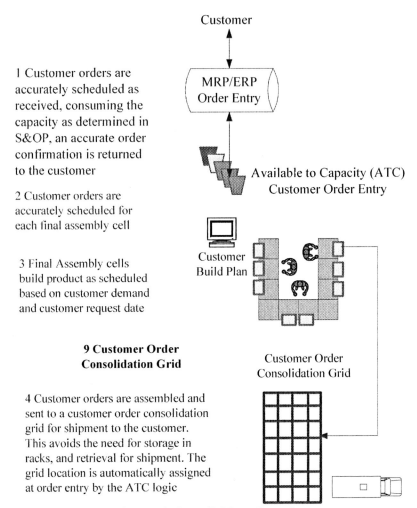

1 Customer orders are accurately scheduled as received, consuming the capacity as determined in S&OP, an accurate order confirmation is returned to the customer

2 Customer orders are accurately scheduled for each final assembly cell

3 Final Assembly cells build product as scheduled based on customer demand and customer request date

Customer

MRP/ERP Order Entry

Available to Capacity (ATC) Customer Order Entry

Customer Build Plan

9 Customer Order Consolidation Grid

Customer Order Consolidation Grid

4 Customer orders are assembled and sent to a customer order consolidation grid for shipment to the customer. This avoids the need for storage in racks, and retrieval for shipment. The grid location is automatically assigned at order entry by the ATC logic

Figure 54: 8 Available to Capacity

As customer orders are booked and scheduled, the order is assigned a customer order consolidation grid number for the purpose of building to a specific date all line items on the order and delivering all line items to a specific location in shipping for final packaging and delivery to the customer.

Building Block 7
Sales & Operations Planning Process Flow

Sales & Operations Planning (S&OP) is a company wide shared forecasted sales plan, whose function is to adjust the supply chain levels of materials and capacity to meet expected customer demand. Participants in the S&OP process generally include operations, sales, engineering, accounting, and management. Other groups can be invited as required.

You will find that committing the time during each monthly financial planning period to participate in the forecast establishment and review is an effective method for communication, and of establishing common goals and plans across the business. This process has the effect of reducing adversarial positions between sales and operations while significantly improving service levels to customers and meeting of financial targets.

Note: Because we are forecasting purchased materials, sub-assemblies, and capacity, and making the necessary supply-chain adjustments, forecast accuracy is not nearly as critical to success as when we attempt to forecast finished goods. Products sold and included in sales planning bills of material require common material to produce. It is this commonality of materials and assemblies that makes the development of forecasting at the family level valid and extremely effective. We forecast at the family level and fill the bins at the component level. When the customer orders, we assemble the components into a product and ship the product, then replace the material as required.

The plant master scheduler should be capable of developing a forecast for the short-term future, based on history. In addition to history, considerations include planned events the master scheduler may not be aware of, such as:

- A planned sales promotion
- Addition of a new sales channel
- Loss of or gain of a major account

■ A new product launch, and the need for pipeline fill or a pre-production run, which consumes capacity.

A typical S&OP flow chart and steps is illustrated and discussed here, with an explanation of the *inputs and outputs* of a successful S&OP processes.

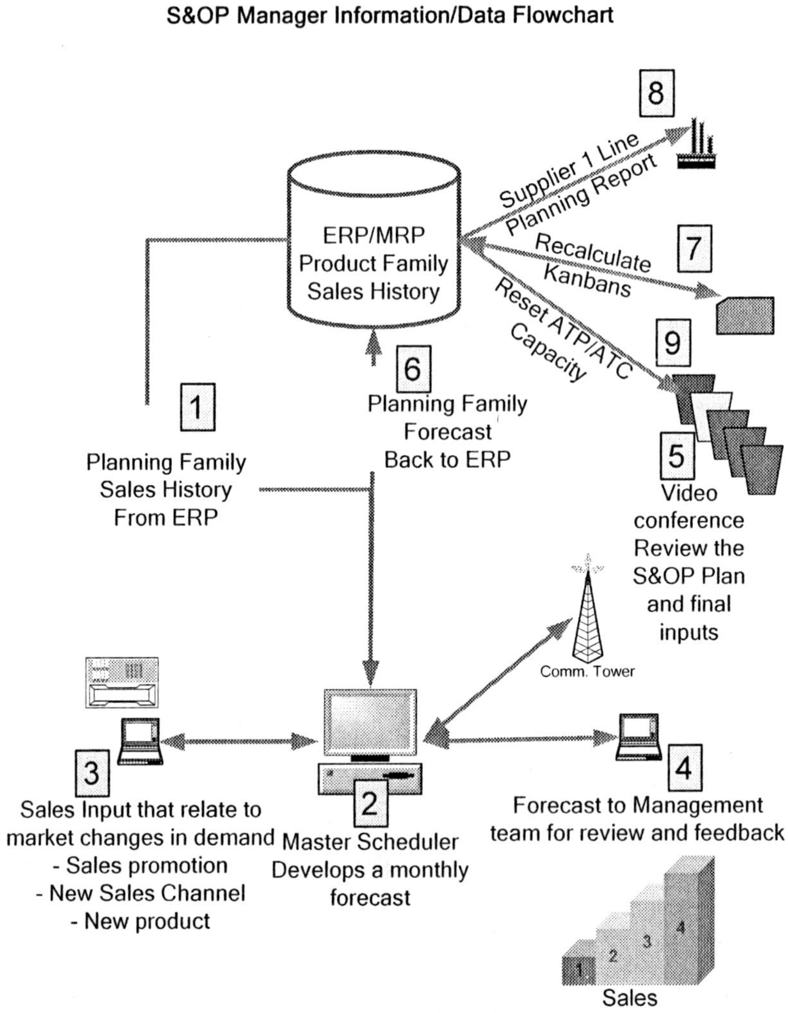

S&OP Manager Information/Data Flowchart

Figure 55: S&OP Manager Information/Data Flowchart

Sales & Operations Planning Steps

1. Planning family history is extracted from MRP/ERP by family.
2. The Master Scheduler develops a forecast using the history and any market intelligence that may be available. The forecast is per planning family, and not for each item sold; however the information regarding a saleable item is readily available. The goal is to forecast at the family level and stock at the component level for final assembly, and at lower levels for supply of product to the final assembly cells.
3. The Master Scheduler seeks sales and engineering input regarding changes in the marketplace, such as those described above.
4. The forecast is calculated and electronically distributed to the S&OP planning team for review prior to the S&OP team review.
5. A video/teleconference S&OP review is conducted with team participation.
6. When agreement on the forecast by planning family is reached, the forecasts, comprised of planning family member percentages, are exported to the MRP/ERP software for forecasting.

Outputs of S&OP

1. When your MRP/ERP has been processed and calculated, the forecasted usage for each kanban part is used to calculate kanban quantities.
2. A supplier 1 line per MRP item purchased part is sent to each supplier for planning purposes.
3. The final assembly cell capacity for each planning family is updated in the ATC cell scheduling software, which resides at order entry on the MRP/ERP software.

Forecast Sales Summary Sheet

The sales forecast sheet is the forecast and history by planning family, for use in the S&OP process and distributed to the S&OP team for review and feedback prior to the team meeting. The information is grouped by:

1. Planning family part #, which is also the planning family name
2. The saleable part number for the planning family (if used)
3. The months of history and forecast shown in the body of the report
4. Information for each planning family in history and forecast for units, sales$, and gross margin $
5. A total for the next 12 months.

Sales Forecast Summary Widgets Family					
History Dates	[3]	May-03	Jun-03	July-03	Aug-03
Forecast Dates		May-04	Jun-04	July-04	Aug-04
Family					
Widget [1] [2]	C3456				
History Pieces:		19765	24657	17654	18769
Forecasted Pieces: [4]		21616	27021	20536	21616
Forecasted Sales $:		148,280	118,640	185,880	221,440
Forecasted Margin $:		66,726	53,388	83,646	99,648
Widget	C3457				
History Pieces:		16987	21376	16548	14356
Forecasted Pieces:		18683	23354	17749	18683
Forecasted Sales $:		1,661,800	1,329,440	2,082,760	2,481,600
Forecasted Margin $:		747,810	598,248	937,242	1,116,720
Widget	C3458				
History Pieces:		13549	16750	12387	14563
Forecasted Pieces:		14432	18040	13711	14432
Forecasted Sales $:		1,256,800	1,005,440	1,575,160	1,876,800
History Pieces:		565,560	452,448	708,822	844,560
12 MONTH GRAND TOTALS:					
History Pieces:		245000			
Forecasted Pieces: [5]		285000			
Forecasted Sales $:		$52,000,000			
Forecasted Margin $:		$21,600,000			

Figure 56: Forecast Sales Summary Sheet

One significant contribution a formalized S&OP process makes to the business is that a unified sales/business plan for the next 12 rolling months is always available. This significantly reduces the time required to develop an annual budget and strategic plan.

Cell Capacity Sheet

The cell Capacity Sheet, is utilized by the master scheduler and the operations manager for the purposes of planning capacity in both cell equipment and in employees.

Cell Summary				
Family	May-04	Jun-04	July-04	Aug-04
Cellname:	20	25 [2]	19	20
Widget Final Assy. [1]				
Pieces Per Day:	2737	2737	2737	2737
Total Forecast:	54732	68415	51995	54732
Monthly Capacity:	80000	80000	120000	120000
Available Capacity: [3]	3328	18663	23905	5504
Forecasted Takt Time:	9.87	9.87	9.87	9.87
Forecast Team/Day:	18	18	18	18
Actual Team/Day:	18	18	18	18
Cellname:				
Widget Sub. Assy.				
Pieces Per Day: [4]	2737	2737	2737	2737
Total Forecast:	54732	68415	51995	229874
Monthly Capacity:	266000	280000	336000	139317
Available Capacity:	35984	95989	47715	-90556
Forecasted Takt Time:	9.87	9.87	9.87	9.87
Forecast Team/Day:	15	15	15 [5]	15
Actual Team/Day:	15	15	15	15
TOTALS:				
Forecast Team/Day: [6]	33	33	33	33
Actual Team/Day:	33	33	33	20

Figure 57: Cell Capacity Sheet

In the example shown, there are six primary pieces of information:

1. The cell and planning family name
2. The months and working days of the months being forecasted
3. Information about the planning family and operations
4. The child second-level forecast for a cell that supplies product to the final assembly cell
5. A noticeable capacity constraint in August 2004, which needs to be discussed with the S&OP team (the forecast is for 229874 units, and the demonstrated capacity is 139317 units, the cell is being retooled for new products.).
6. The forecasted and actual team sizes, displayed for information in determining changes required.

ATC Capacity Input for Customer Order Scheduling

Available to Capacity (ATC) will be defined in more detail later in this section of the book; however, it is important to link the S&OP output for cell capacity planning to ATC. As will be explained in the ATC section, cell capacity as determined at S&OP will be used in customer order booking to match capacity to demand. This process prevents unintentional over booking of capacity in the production final assembly cells.

We know from the S&OP planning example above that we are forecasting to sell 2737 Widgets per day for May 2004 and that we have committed to produce that quantity per day. Capacity for the Widget final assembly cell has been established as 2737/day, or for a 5-day working week, 13685/week. The 13685 units/week is the Widget final assembly cell capacity for a planned 5 day work week. This capacity is used by ATC for scheduling of customer orders.

Supplier 1 Line per Item MRP Planning Report

The supplier 1 line per item planning report is extracted directly from the MRP/ERP software, after the forecast has been entered and MRP/ERP processed. The report is formatted by supplier and can be sent in a digital file, or posted to a website or as an attachment to an email.

Supplier 1 Line MRP Report ☐3

Supplier Identification	JIT INC. ☐1		Assemble to Order Inc. ☐2				Date		04/26/04
Contact:	ronw@JITINC.com			Contact:	Diane I want it on time				diane@jit.com

Family Assembly/Part #	Kanban Quantity	02-May	09-May ☐5	16-May	23-May	Jun-04 ☐6	Jul-04	Aug-04	Total Units
2349 ☐4	19000	19000	19000	19000	19000	76000	98800	118560	369360
12435	19000	19000	19000	19000	19000	76000	98800	118560	369360
ghuy67	10000	10000	10000	10000	10000	40000	52000	62400	194400
fgt678	7500	7500	7500	7500	7500	30000	39000	46800	145800
fr657	950	950	950	950	950	3800	4940	5928	18468
ghu87	950	950	950	950	950	3800	4940	5928	18468
efd6543	950	950	950	950	950	3800	4940	5928	18468
Totals		58350	58350	58350	58350	233400	303420	364104	1134324

Figure 58: MRP Planning Report

The supplier 1 line per item report is used to reduce the lead time from a supplier by giving the supplier sufficient information to plan production and reduce their lead time to that of packaging and shipping time once a release has been triggered.

The supplier 1 line report contains:

1. Contact information from the ordering contact
2. The supplier contact information
3. The date of the report
4. Part #s being ordered and the kanban quantity
5. The planned quantity for the next few weeks, and for the next few months.

This report is sent to suppliers weekly, or when a major change in the business occurs that affects the suppliers.

Building Block 8
ATC Customer Order Scheduling

ATC, Available to Capacity, is a primary route of the overall Lean Roadmap process. ATC is the capacity management process at order entry that allows for:

■ Scheduling of customer orders to final assembly cell capacity for repetitive products
■ Full lead-time scheduling of cells for non-repetitive items
■ Prevention of over-scheduling of cells at the time of order booking. Scheduling that exceeds capacity is done when a known on-time delivery will occur.

ATC Process Flow

ATC is a final assembly capacity matching process. As orders are received, capacity is reduced in the cell for the week the product is requested.

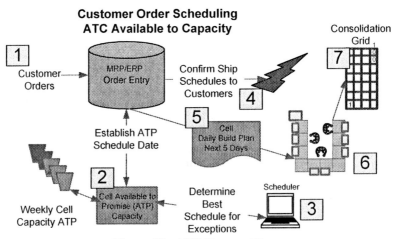

Figure 59: ATC Process Flow

A more detailed description of the process is:

1. As customer orders are received,
2. Orders are compared against a capacity table for available capacity. (Note that all line items on an order are considered and the longest lead-time date for the order is used for the delivery date.)
3. Should an order promise date exceed the customer requested date, a best date is determined by the scheduler and the customer is notified.
4. Customers receive an immediate order confirmation for those orders that meet or are less than promised lead-time, and a confirmation is given for dates that are greater than the customer requested date.
5. A daily customer build schedule is used by each cell leader to macro-schedule the cell for that day or week, and plan staffing levels based on calculated Takt time.
6. Customer orders are assembled and labeled for delivery to a specific order consolidation point.
7. Assembled products are delivered multiple times per day to a specific customer order consolidation point for shipment.

Customer Order Scheduling

ATC Available to Capacity

Each bucket represents one production week,
Each bucket of capacity = a weekly capacity of 13685 units of product.

Notes of Clarification

1. The ATC module is a macro-scheduling tool and is divided into weekly capacity buckets for each final assembly cell. Each bucket contains a quantity of units that can be produced per day times the number of working days scheduled for that week.

2. A weighted average cycle time at the constraint operation, based on sales and operations planning logic, is used to calculate unit capacity.

3. The final cell is where the micro-scheduling takes place. At ATC, a promise date for the last workday of the week the product is scheduled is promised. (This is variable.)   Therefore   the   cell   has   not   been overscheduled.   The cell leader then groups work together based on assembly logic, and by customer request date all customer orders are grouped on the customer build schedule by date and part number.

4. Takt times are calculated each week and/or day for each cell, providing the cell leader an indication of staffing required to meet the customer demand. Standardized work sheets are then used to assign work within the cell.

5. In the Lean Roadmap process, material for assembly of repetitive products is not considered as a constraint. Lean Roadmap uses the same number of family units forecasted to plan capacity and to plan kanban levels. For non-repetitive items, Lean Roadmap first verifies any available finished goods inventory. If none exists then the end-to-end lead-time for the product from MRPII is used to schedule the cell, consume the capacity, and promise the order.

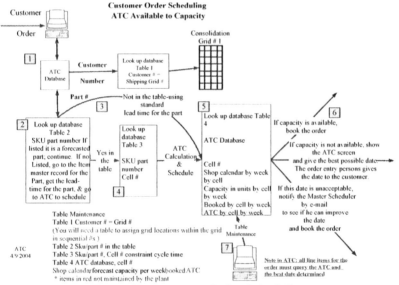

Figure 60: Customer Order Scheduling

ATC Customer Order Scheduling Logic

The ATC logic is easy to understand. Scheduling an assemble-to-order cell is a matter of simple subtraction.

1. The ATC database uses the part number to access a lookup table.
2. If the part number is in the table, the product is a repetitive item and is forecasted.
3. If the part number is not in the table but is active, then finished goods inventory is checked. If none is available, the standard lead time for the product is used in the scheduling table for the final assembly cell.
4. The second table is the part number to cell relationship, where the product is assembled.
5. The third table is for scheduling, in the week requested.
6. A number of outcomes are defined in the illustration: capacity available/unavailable.

149

7. The plant Master Scheduler maintains the ATC capacity, and product tables and database.

Customer Cell Build Schedule & Takt Time

The Cell Build Schedule (dispatch list) is printed or viewed from the MRPII database. In a just-in-time environment, it is not unusual for the cell leader to view the requirements several times per day, based upon the backlog the company experiences.

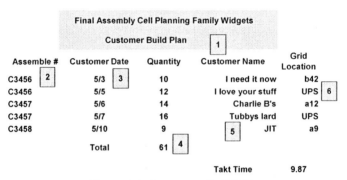

Assemble #	Customer Date	Quantity	Customer Name	Grid Location
C3456	5/3	10	I need it now	b42
C3456	5/5	12	I love your stuff	UPS
C3457	5/6	14	Charlie B's	a12
C3457	5/7	16	Tubbys lard	UPS
C3458	5/10	9	JIT	a9
Total		61		

Takt Time   9.87

Figure 61: Customer Build Plan

The cell build schedule must display at least basic information for the cell:

1. The cell name
2. The part numbers required—sorted by date and part number to allow the cell leader to group product for the most efficient build sequence
3. The customer request date. The request date always take precedence over cell assembly efficiency in grouping. **The scheduling done in the cell is micro-scheduling. I have yet to find a computer algorithm or scheduler who schedules on a micro basis better than a cell leader**.
4. The quantity required for each order

5. The customer name. This is important to the cell associates; they can relate to a customer name.

6. The customer order consolidation grid location. This is a physical location on the floor in shipping where this customer's orders (coming from several cells/locations) are consolidated for shipment.

Building Block 9
Customer Order Consolidation Grid Logic

The customer order consolidation grid is a logic that assigns a customer (ship to) address or specific requirement for shipping to a grid location in the shipping department.

Traditional manufacturing build-to-ship processes include a few steps that follow a logic of build, store on a storage rack shelf, remove from the rack shelf, consolidate, pack, ship. The Lean Roadmap logic skips the storage rack steps. **Note: Our goal is to remove racks, eliminate finished goods inventory, and convert the space to productive use.**

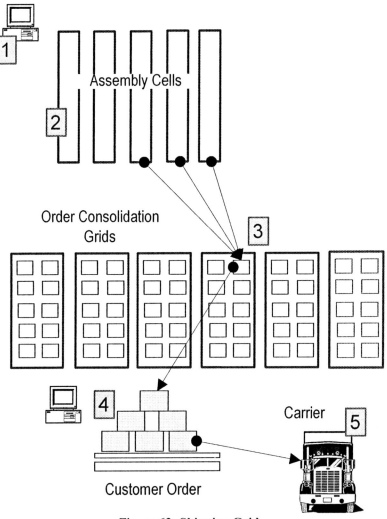

Figure 62: Shipping Grid

The shipping grid logic is quite simple:

1. At the time of order entry, a shipping grid location is assigned to the customer order for each line on the order.

2. Each assembly cell reads a dispatch list and builds the product to customer order date. This means that several cells can all be working on the same order/different lines, but all working to the same date. The products are built by customer order line, and a deliver-to-grid-location label is affixed to each container/product built and placed in the cell outbound location. The customer order/work order is closed, the order is "backflushed" in MRPII, and accounting records for inventory, labor, and overhead are satisfied.

3. The product is delivered to the appropriate grid location several times per day. As the products are received into the grid, the customer order line item is received into finished goods inventory at the appropriate location.

4. The customer order is completed, packaged, and digitally removed from inventory. The delivery carrier has already been notified or the docked trailer loaded (being one of the grid locations).

5. The product is shipped and invoiced.

Note that grids are generally route and carrier specific, so an analysis of your current shipping logistics is required.

The following illustration gives additional detail as to how the shipping-grid order-consolidation logic functions. Table 4 assigns a customer ship-to to a specific consolidation grid location. Table 5 shows a sequential logic by grid. As customer orders are booked, each sequential order for a particular grid is assigned the next grid location, generally 1-10. When the last order is received and assigned to position 10 in grid/route 2, the next grid/route 2 sales order goes to position 1.

The logic follows steps 1-5:

1. Book the order.
2. Determine if the customer location has been assigned a grid/route location. If so select it.
3. An override to select an overnight carrier is available.

4. Assign the grid-to-customer relationship.
5. Assign the grid/route location for order consolidation.

Customer Order Consolidation Grid

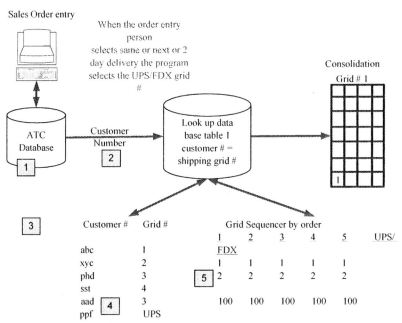

Figure 63: Customer Order Consolidation Grid

Building Block 10
Kanban

Process Overview

Kanban, as defined here, is a closed-loop process for assuring the timely replacement of repetitively consumed inventory. A kanban location is an inventory location for an item, with a unit quantity for that item based on sales and operations planning forecast for the saleable products that use the item and the lead-time required to replace the kanban units. The intent of a kanban location for a part is the elimination of the natural lead-time required for that part. Establishing a kanban location makes the part available for consumption based on customer demand.

Thus kanbans are fixed-order quantity items based on a reorder point and reorder quantity, no different than traditional MRPII logic with two important exceptions:

1. Kanbans are recalculated monthly after the sales and operations planning (S&OP) process, and the fixed-order quantity is automatically updated in the item/inventory master field for the part, thus making the reorder quantity in your MRP/ERP software correct based on the business forecast and part lead-time.
2. Kanban quantities are reordered based on customer consumption, and the person doing the reordering is the person who removes the parts from the kanban location.

The kanban process is a natural and required ingredient of lean manufacturing, allowing the management and replenishment of inventory to be controlled at the point of use. This process dramatically reduces the stock-outs normally encountered with traditional inventory management methods. Kanban becomes an integral part of your MRP/ERP/DRP software, and provides a powerful way to leverage your investment in a lean environment.

Kanban Calculation Process

The following figure is a simplified flow for the adjustment of kanbans after S&OP, or given that a change in business levels has occurred or is expected to occur.

1. A planning family forecast is agreed upon at S&OP, and that forecast is loaded into the MRPII processor forecast for a planning family.
2. MRPII/ERP processes and calculates the greater of forecast or sales orders for all products and components and assemblies required.

3. Kanbans are recalculated based on the latest S&OP forecast, based on average planned daily usage and numbers of days lead-time required for replenishment.
4. Kanbans quantities are adjusted to meet the new required quantities.
5. Suppliers are sent an electronic Supplier 1 line per Part Planning Report that includes the new kanban quantity for the part.

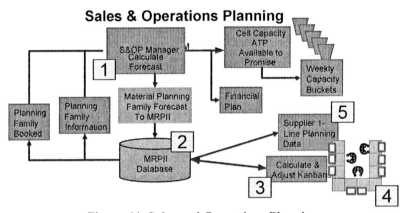

Figure 64: Sales and Operations Planning

As a note of reference, some MRPII software packages have built in kanban processes. For those of you who do not have that luxury; there are commercially available packages that connect to your MRPII software, such as **Kanban Manager™.**

The Kanban Process
Information and Material Flow

The following diagram is a graphic flow of the kanban card and of the material, in a manual system. Let me pre-qualify my reason for showing and explaining a manual ordering process.

1. I advise you to do your first kanban cell manually. Establishing a manual kanban for one cell is very

simple. Once the process is in place, make the changes, enhancements, and improvements desired, document the process, and then automate the process.

2. Many businesses do not have the infrastructure to automate the kanban processes. I am referring to barcode scanning, automatic notification to the internal cells via computer of a kanban requirement, automatic notification to external suppliers via e-mail, or another Internet protocol for a kanban replenishment.

3. Learning how to manage kanbans manually will give you the opportunity to hone your process, train employees, and further improve the process with little delay. An automated process that has waste and poor process definition designed into it is much more difficult to repair.

Here's an example of the logical manual flow steps for the material and kanban card for a purchased and manufactured part:

Purchased Part -- the Dotted Line

1. A kanban card for a purchased item is placed in the kanban pickup box located at the final assembly cell.
2. The material handler makes routine stops at the cell and picks up the card for delivery to purchasing.
3. Purchasing looks at the MRPII requirements to determine if any adjustments are required, then places a release with the supplier and enters the release into the MRPII/ERP software. The kanban card is placed on the kanban schedule board at receiving, or returned to the cell with order information on the back of the card. Each day, at the end of the first shift, the receiving department alerts purchasing for any kanbans that were due that day and not received. Receiving should use an open purchase order report by due date for this process.
4. The supplier ships the required products.
5. The product is received, and MRPII/ERP records are updated at receiving.

6. The product and kanban card are grouped.
7. The material handler delivers the product and kanban card to the cell. Note: An alternate was for the kanban card to have been returned to the cell after the product was ordered.

Manufactured Item -- The Solid Line

1. A kanban card for a manufactured item is placed in the kanban pickup box located at the final assembly cell.
2. The material handler delivers the card to the supplier cell. I have eliminated the need for a planner and or work order, as bills of material are flattened and scheduling for the supplier cell is done at the cell.
3. The internal supplier-cell schedules the cell and produces the item.
4. The material handler delivers the item and the kanban card back to the cell.

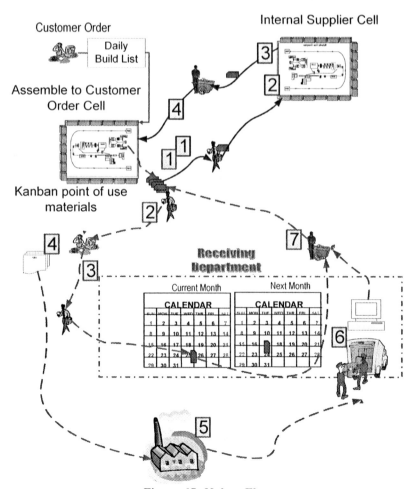

Figure 65: Kaban Flow

For common usage kanban material—material that is routinely consumed by several locations—it is advisable to establish a common material storage location for these kanbans. The material stored in the cell at point of use is a fixed quantity, which you can determine based on part size and value. The quantity stored in the common kanban storage location is the quantity that is recalculated monthly and is the quantity that is replenished as a kanban.

Note: Lean Roadmap calculates both kanban levels and final assembly cell capacity at S&OP, and then uses the cell capacity ATC at order entry to schedule cells to capacity. Thus the supply chain is not overscheduled, and is in equilibrium.

For materials that are consumed in more than one location, a common material storage area works well.

This eliminates multiple cards traveling from several consumption points to the supplier.

Figure 66: Common Material Storage Supply Chain

Kanban Calculations

Kanban is a reorder point—reorder quantity method of inventory replenishment. Understanding the calculations and keeping them simple is of primary importance. Keep in mind that in Lean Roadmap, one of the primary performance measurements is the elimination or significant reduction of finished goods inventory, replaced with kanbans located at strategic points in the process, such as final assembly cells and internal supplier cells. Kanbans at strategic process points with correctly calculated values support quick response to customers.

Kanbans are inventory and effectively eliminate the lead-time required to obtain them, as they are present in the form of a kanban. When we replace finished goods inventory with raw and work-in-process kanbans, we see a significant reduction in the inventory investment required, and a tremendous leveraging of working capital to improve customer on-time delivery.

As you have learned in the previous sections of this book, planning family forecasts are utilized in S&OP to calculate both kanban sizes and final assembly cell capacity ATC. The fact that ATC is used to balance and match demand and capacity also reduces the risk of draining the supply chain of material.

With this information in mind we now consider simple kanban calculations for both internal and external suppliers. Note that there are many sophisticated and detailed calculations for kanbans, and additional information that you require is readily available using the Internet and textbooks.

Internal Kanbans

The devil is in the details; in the classic accounting approach, the term EOQ (economic order quantity) is used to determine lot size based on comparing set-up costs to inventory carrying costs. This calculation and its use dates back to a time when inventory was a good thing, and maximizing equipment was a good thing. In today's world of lean, my advice is to minimize lot/kanban sizes by reducing set-up times. It is not a bad thing to reduce lot sizes even with excessive set-up times, given that the machine capacity is available to do so.

In the following example, you can work the math from the example. The important elements to note are:

1. Set-up time drives a kanban quantity of 2830 pieces, and with no set-up time, the kanban quantity is 25. Somewhere between these two numbers is a good kanban quantity, until the set-up times are addressed.
2. The kanban calculation for a manufactured item is the greater of the EOQ (reduced by common sense) and the calculation of the expected average daily usage for the part multiplied by the replenishment lead-time for the part, plus safety days, added to the replenishment lead-

time days. This figure is rounded up to the next order multiple/package quantity.

Replenishment Lead-Time Days = the lead-time as determined from a value stream mapping event that eliminates all of the non-value added wait times in the conventional process. For an internal supplier, it is not uncommon to experience replenishment lead-time days of 1-3.

Example:

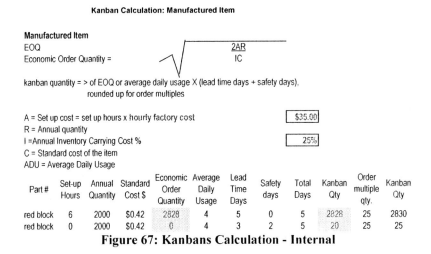

Kanban Calculation: Manufactured Item

Manufactured Item
EOQ
Economic Order Quantity =

$$\sqrt{\frac{2AR}{IC}}$$

kanban quantity = > of EOQ or average daily usage X (lead time days + safety days), rounded up for order multiples

A = Set up cost = set up hours x hourly factory cost $35.00
R = Annual quantity
I =Annual Inventory Carrying Cost %   25%
C = Standard cost of the item
ADU = Average Daily Usage

Part #	Set-up Hours	Annual Quantity	Standard Cost $	Economic Order Quantity	Average Daily Usage	Lead Time Days	Safety days	Total Days	Kanban Qty	Order multiple qty.	Kanban Qty
red block	6	2000	$0.42	2828	4	5	0	5	2828	25	2830
red block	0	2000	$0.42	0	4	3	2	5	20	25	25

Figure 67: Kanbans Calculation - Internal

External (Purchased) Kanbans

For external kanbans there are two major differences from the internal kanbans:

1. No calculation for EOQ is used; however, the supplier may have an order quantity in mind that is negotiable.
2. Replenishment lead-time is understood to be the time it takes for package and shipment of the material ordered. There are a few qualifiers to this statement:

A supplier one-line planning report must be used to allow the supplier to plan and be prepared.

A supplier Just-in-Time Lean agreement must be in place, with the supplier being certified by history as being reliable both in quality and delivery, and preferably utilizing an ongoing continuous improvement process.

Repetitive material from half way around the world with weekly deliveries required will require a logistics plan for the boat-to-boat, plane-to-plane kanban calculations and scheduling.

Replenishment Lead-Time Days = the lead-time as determined from a value stream mapping event that eliminates all of the non-value added wait times, purchasing, and manufacturing lead-times in the process. For an external supplier, it is not uncommon to experience replenishment lead-time days of 1-5 for domestic suppliers.

Example:

Kanban Calculation: Purchased Item

Purchased Item
kanban quantity = average daily usage X (lead time days + safety days), rounded up to agree with order multiples

A = Set up cost = set up hours x hourly factory cost $35.00

R = Annual quantity

I =Annual Inventory Carrying Cost % 25%

C = Standard cost of the item

ADU = Average Daily Usage

Part #	Annual Quantity	Standard Cost $	Average Daily Usage	Lead Time Days	Safety days	Total Days	Kanban Qty	Order multiple qty	Kanban Qty
red block	2000	$0.42	4	5	0	5	20	25	25

Figure 68: Kanban Calculation - External

Kanban Design Steps

Select an area and items to convert to kanban.
Select a predictable process.

■ Design the kanban pull system Material and Information Flow Value Stream Maps
■ Calculate kanbans.
■ Train employees and ask for ideas.
■ Organize the cell for point-of-use inventory.
■ Try the process, and adjust as necessary.
■ Define a replenishment process with your suppliers (internal or external).

Considerations for Kanban Implementation

■ Assemble to Customer Order Logic being used Flattened Bills of Material & Routings
■ System Backflushing of Material & Labor
■ System-Generated Calculations and Kanban Cards

Supplier One-Page MRP Planning Report
■ Supplier Point-of-Use Inventory Maintenance
■ Supplier Consigned Inventory determined and available

Performance Measurements in Place
■ Database Accuracy: Bills of material, lead-times, inventory
■ Inventory: Bills of Material, Routings, Work Centers
■ Include Available to Capacity & Scheduling at Order Entry
■ Planning Bills for Forecasting & Planning.

Advantages of Kanban Implementation

■ System is visible (Kanban = a visual method of triggering replenishment (usually a card, bin, or level meter)
■ Distributed control systems where complex system behavior is controlled by simple rules
■ Visual controls reduce the need for expediting
■ More time to concentrate on high $ items, cost reduction, lead-time reduction, and supply-line consolidation

■ Replacement is based on demand
■ Cornerstone of Just-in-Time Manufacturing
■ Significantly reduces inventory levels
■ Inventory is converted to cash, creating a stronger and better-leveraged business, with more resources to invest in new products, systems, marketing.

Suppliers: Extension of Your Business Capability

Suppliers are an extension of your current manufacturing capability. They are an ally, not an enemy. Very often a supplier is viewed as a poor resource, when in reality, they have been offered poor, inaccurate, or no information regarding your needs and goals.

Take the time required to meet with your suppliers for the purpose of design of a lean supply chain. Suppliers have additional resources, capabilities, and good ideas for improvement of delivery, inventory levels, and cost; however, we are generally too busy to discuss these topics with a goal of improving the supply chain management process and overall cost of doing business. Solicit their input and lessons-learned information.

Suppliers are also businesspeople, and should realize that the trading relationship being established will be long and profitable, if the supplier remains the high-quality, short lead-time, competitive resource required to compete in the marketplace. This requirement places much of the performance burden on the supplier; the relationship will endure given that the supplier continues to meet the qualifications as defined and agreed upon.

Defining the Business Relationship and Requirements

Suppliers want to know, and need to know, what you expect from them. Think this through carefully, in view of the supply chain value stream map, and establish a rationale for the importance of each expectation.

When you initially discuss the lean supply chain process with your top two or three suppliers and roll out the information flow, material flow, and conditions of doing business, be sure to take off your manufacturing hat—they will never agree to this attitude—and put on your sales hat. Place yourself in the position of your supplier. A supplier wants to maintain your business, and if the new process is reasonable and well-thought-out, then there is a high probability of acceptance and input from them.

Suppliers have a keen interest in the health of your business—your business is doing the marketing, design, and selling; the supplier gets to enjoy incremental income as a result of doing business with you.

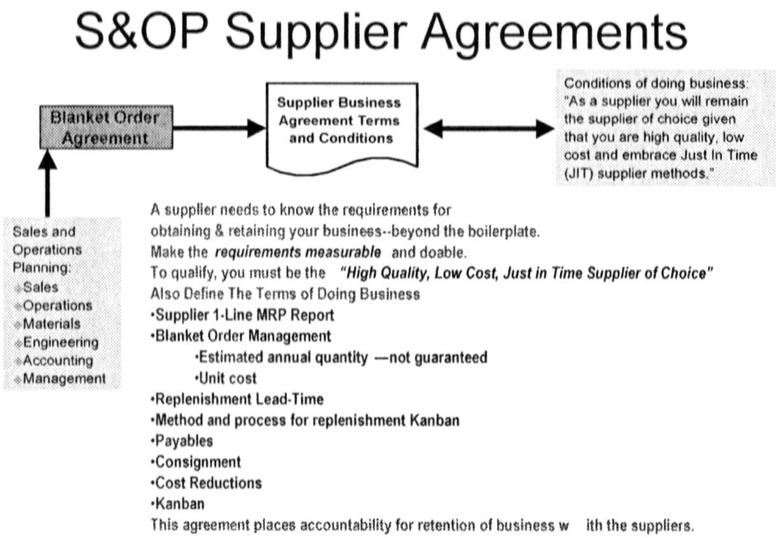

S&OP Supplier Agreements

Figure 69: Supplier Agreements

New Product Introduction Process

Looking at your profit and loss statement and your balance sheet, you should see that purchased material and inventory are the very near the top in dollar value. Suppliers are a tremendous resource for introducing products that reflect lowest cost, shortest lead-time, and product standardization. During the product design process, your engineering department should be maintaining a costed BOM, and have knowledge regarding the current gross margin % for the product.

Obtaining supplier input throughout the design process will assure the best result in measurements of quality, lead-time, and cost. Once you and a couple of your key suppliers have completed the future state VSM process for management of the value stream, document the process, cut it in, and measure the results.

Lean Roadmap Information Flow Logic

The following tables illustrate the flow of information and calculations required in Lean Roadmap. In essence the sales history in units, used to calculate the sales forecast in units, routing sequence and standard cycle time, ATC Cell Manager, ATC Order Scheduling Manager, and the Cell Customer Build Schedule.

The process evolves in the following steps:

1. Sales history in units per model within the product planning family is retrieved.
2. A sales forecast for the family is developed based on history and market intelligence.
3. The routing sequence and cycle times from standardized work is used to determine capacity required to meet the forecast.
4. The ATC cell Manager is adjusted to meet required capacity, this information is used in the ATC Scheduling table of Order Manager for scheduling customer orders in weekly buckets of capacity.
5. The ATC customer order table is utilized at order entry to properly schedule customer orders with regard to requested date and cell capacity.
6. The cell customer build schedule is then reviewed by each cell at least daily to plan manning to Takt time, and proper build sequence.

2 Planning Family Widgets	History Sold 1			3 Total Units Sold	% of Total Sold	Average/ day sold
	O-03	N-04	D-04			
	20	18	24			
C3456	21659	19876	25476	67011	39.5%	1081
C3457	18721	17654	21543	57918	34.1%	934
C3458	14543	12543	17654	44740	26.4%	722
Totals	54923	50073	64673	169669	100%	2737
Average Units/Day	2,746	2,782	2,695	2,737	4	

Figure 70: Sales History

1. The sales history for product planning family A.
2. The specific product planning family, for which there may be several for this cell.
3. The product planning family model number, units sold, and % of the total planning family.
4. The average units sold per day, monthly and in total.

	Forecast			1		
2	**May-04**	**Jun-04**	**Jul-04**	**Aug-04**	**Total**	
Planning Family Widgets	20	25	19	20 **3**	84	**Average/ day forecasted**
C3456	21616	27021	20536	21616	90789	1081
C3457	18683	23354	17749	18683	78470	934
C3458	14432	18040	13711	14432	60615	722
Sales Forecast	54732	68415	51995	54732	229874	2737
Average Units/Day	2737	2737	2737	2737	2737 **4**	

Figure 71: Sales Forecast

1. The sales forecast for the next 4 month period.
2. The forecast is for planning family A.
3. Model numbers included in the forecast.
4. Level loaded planning units/day.

Routing Sequence and Standard Cycle Time

Using a flattened routing (all final assembly operations as part of the final assembly cell expressed as one routing step) as defined in standardized work, the second table shows forecasted quantity of units for an assembly, multiplied by the demonstrated routing-step time for the family member using a sum product logic, then divided by the total units forecasted. Thus the weighted average station cycle time for all products in the cell is determined, the total time is determined for manning purposes, and the constraint is identified for capacity scheduling. The Takt time was determined knowing the customer forecast and hours that the cell is scheduled to work. The forecasted Takt time from each station is divided into the weighted average cycle time for each station to determine the number of stations required to meet Takt time.

Widget Final Assembly, Test & Package Cell

PPQ Level 1 Final Assembly Routing Sequence and Standard Cycle Time

[1] Operation Work Ctrs	Step 1	Step 2	Step 3	Step 4	Step 5	Step 6	Total
Planning Family Widgets Set Up Hrs.	0.00	0.00	0.00	0.00	0.00	0.00	0.00
C3456 Cycle Times	30	[2] 27	29	26	31	27	170
C3457 Seconds	31	29	32	27	36	29	184
C3458	33	32	36	29	39	32	201
[3] Weighted Avg Times	31	29	32	27	[4] 35	29	183
[5] Forecasted Takt Time Seconds	9.87	9.87	9.87	9.87	9.87	9.87	
[6] Stations Required	3.2	2.9	3.2	2.8	3.5	2.9	18.5

Figure 72: Routing Sequence

1. The operation sequence in the final assembly cell as defined by standardized work, cut and assembly through pack.
2. The standard hours for each model in the product planning family (highlighted), in this case three models.
3. The weighted average cycle time for each operation, this is the product of the quantity forecasted for each model for the four months times the standard hours for each model for each operation in the final assembly cell.
4. The constraint cycle time in the cell has been identified as test. The quantity scheduled per period will be paced by the test operation cycle time.
5. Forecasted Takt time for each operation in the cell is calculated.
6. The number of stations is calculated (weighted average time/Takt time) for each operation. In this case 18.5 operators/stations are required to meet the forecasted demand. Referring to the standardized work sheet for this assembly cell, the manning assignments will be revealed.

Cell Manager Planning table, that is maintained by the Master Scheduler, showing the following variables to be maintained:

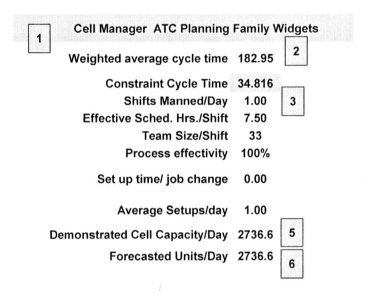

Figure 73: Cell Manager Planning Table

1. The ATC Cell Manager table for Family A final assembly cell. This table is adjusted each time S&OP is calculated for ATC management at customer order entry.
2. The weighted average cycle time for the family.
3. The constraints weighted average cycle time for the family.
4. Average planned/demonstrated set up/changeovers per day.
5. The demonstrated cell capacity per day.
6. The forecasted units per day.

In the case of this example, the forecasted units per day is slightly higher than the demonstrated capacity, and in all likelihood poses no problem for planning at that level.

ATC Scheduling Table at Customer Order Entry

The ATC table simply shows the weekly capacity in units, using weighted average cycle time at the constraint, and capacity to determine that this cell can produce 2737 units per week. The table then has a booked quantity for the week, and an ATC capacity for each week. Each week's capacity is equal to the shop calendar days for the week, times the unit capacity for a day. The table is updated and utilized in the background, and only displays when capacity has been exceeded, or when the customer requests a date for delivery as a question rather than a firm order.

ATC Scheduling Table Planning Family Widgets				
1	**May-04**	**Jun-04**	**Jul-04**	**Aug-04**
Cell ATC Capacity/day	2,736.6	2,736.6	2,736.6	2,736.6
3 Forecast/day	2,736.6	2,736.6	2,736.6	2,736.6
Monthly Capacity	54,732	68,415	51,995	54,732
Forecasted Takt Time	9.866	9.866	9.866	9.866
Booked wk 1	2,876	243	3	2
ATC wk 1	10,807	13,440	13,680	13,681
Booked wk 2	598	58	6	0
ATC wk 2	13,085	13,625	13,677	13,683
Booked wk 3	543	43	8	0
ATC wk 3	13,140	13,640	13,675	13,683
Booked wk 4	387	45	0	0
ATC wk 4	13,296	13,638	13,683	13,683
Booked wk 5	0	34	0	0
ATC wk 5	0	13,649	0	
Total Booked	4,404	423	17	2
Total Capacity	54,732	68,415	51,995	54,732

Figure 74: Scheduling Table

1. The ATC Available to Capacity table for Family A cell.
2. The cell Available to Capacity daily capacity in units.
3. Forecasted units/day.
4. The monthly capacity in units.
5. The forecasted Takt time.
6. The ATC table itself, the number of units booked by week.
7. The Available to Capacity units left to promise/book by week.
8. The total booked/available capacity in units for the four months.

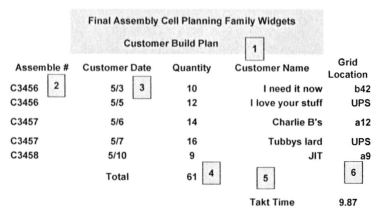

Figure 75: Customer Build Plan

1. The build schedule plan for planning family A in Cell A.
2. The date and model number required.
3. The quantity required.
4. The total units on order and not build for the period of time the report has been run for.
5. The customer name.
6. The Order consolidation grid location where the product is to be delivered to.

That's all there is to it. A very logical straightforward process for supply chain planning and management. The **planning** is derived in S&OP, capacity, kanban sized, ATC final cell capacity, and planning information for suppliers. The management is utilizing ATC at customer order entry, matching demand to capacity, and in kanban replenishment.

The Lean Roadmap process is most effective when we keep it "simple".

MRP/ERP and Lean

I have seen more than my share of poor MRPII/ERP implementations, and subsequent database destructions over time, than I care to remember. It is a requirement that the current or planned database be accurate.

Database Cleanup

Undertake as part of the lean implementation a review of the company database and correction of data in the:

- Bills of material structures
- Lead-times (replenishment)
- Inventory accuracy
- Customer master files in MRP/RP
- Supplier master files in MRP/ERP
- Work orders and purchase orders

Lean Software

Lean software functionality is required for most MRPII/ERP installations. This software is commercially available, items such as **Kanban Manager™,** and **Sales and Operations Manager™.** The available to promise **Order Manager™** is a program logic written for your business and integrated within your business software.

Traditional MRP/ERP software packages will not generally support the Lean Roadmap process, or lean in general. Not to offend the software suppliers, recently some of the packages have added some lean functionality, however asking for a suggested business Lean Roadmap is advisable.

Barcode scanning is an absolute must for Lean Roadmap. In a build/assemble to order world the transactions are significantly increased. Each customer order = a work order for each line item (opened at order entry, closed in the cell). There are more material receipts with Kanban as lead times are significantly reduced and order frequency with smaller lot/Kanban sizes is increased.

Continuous Improvement

The continuous improvement process guarantees that the good work and improvements made in the cell implementation are maintained and continuously improved upon. A closed-loop process of waste identification and elimination of non-value added activity guarantees that the cell performance measurements will improve over time.

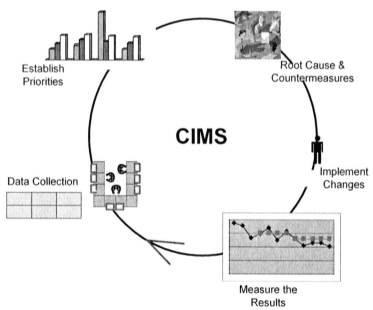

Figure 76: Continuous Improvement

The basic continuous improvement steps are:

1. Collect data. Data collection is performed and posted by cell associates, with a frequency that matches the cycle time: hourly, daily, and weekly.
2. Establish priorities. The cell leader completes a Pareto chart, meets with the technical support team, and together they determine the priorities to be worked on.

3. Determine root causes. The technical team determines root cause of the non-value added activities, countermeasures for corrective action, and an implementation schedule.
4. Implement the changes, and record the results.

Continuous improvement is a disciplined, repetitive process that requires a special skill-set to oversee the management of the factory progress. I suggest the quality manager be assigned the responsibility for design, implementation, and maintenance of the continuous improvement process.

Conclusion

I hope you have found the truly *new* concepts of **Lean Roadmap** useful in your business improvement process. These include:

1. Sales & Operations Planning outputs
   a. Product planning families
   b. Automatic calculation of planning bill percentages
   c. Supplier 1-line planning
   d. ATC capacity establishment
2. ATC (available to capacity) Matching of demand to capacity at order entry, eliminating the need for post MRP infinite capacity rescheduling
3. Customer order consolidation grid. Say goodbye to finished goods racks.

I wrote this book for you, in the hope that it will make your implementation of JIT Lean successful. Over the years of my career I have had the pleasure to work with many dedicated and sincere people who have struggled with the complexity of business design and simplification, while managing the day-to-day operation and planning for the future.

I urge you to take the time to carefully read and understand the **11 Lean Roadmap Building Blocks**. Knowledge is power, and it is this knowledge of the basic lean building blocks that will convert your business to a and considerably more efficient one that improves how customers, shareholders, suppliers, and employees evaluate and enjoy working with the business.

Everything that is worth achieving carries a related cost in effort. Achieving a superior Lean Roadmap design and implementation will be directly proportional to your effort in understanding the building blocks, designing the processes for your business, seeing through an implementation, and sticking with the plan until the new way of processing information and material becomes accepted and ingrained as part of the culture.

Good luck!
Howard

GLOSSARY OF TERMS

ATC, Available to Capacity Customer Order Management/Scheduling. A process for accurately scheduling customer order demand to final assembly cell capacity, and alerting the customer service representative when capacity is not available in the period. This is an output of the sales and operations planning process, and is the key to on-time delivery to the customer, and to removing the havoc created by business software that books customer orders to infinite capacity. The capacity bucket size per week in units is derived from the S&OP output. This capacity is determined for each 5-day period based on the working days for that period and the schedule/day. This is simply expressed as units per week capacity. As customer service representatives book sales, the capacity for that week is consumed. Any order that cannot meet the required date (for all order line items) is immediately flagged for personal attention.

ATP, Available to Promise. A term used by software suppliers to refer to a process of comparing the requirements in material to fill a specific customer order item at a specific time with available capacity and specific material used in the product.

Backflushing. A process used by MRP/ERP software suppliers to eliminate work-in-process inventory transactions and use only raw/purchased level and finished goods transactions. When an order for a finished goods product is completed and issued to inventory, all items required in the bill of material are moved within the general ledger and inventory accounts from raw/purchased to finished goods. Additionally, any labor and overhead is applied to the value of the finished goods item, and all general ledger accounts for these items is updated.

BOM/Bill of Material Structure. A listing of material required to manufacture one unit of product. The listing of material is organized in the logical sequence of build, listing each subassembly and the material to make that subassembly. The bill of material lists the final assembly part # and all required material needed to make 1 unit, and the quantity for each item. This is repeated for all assemblies and material required to make the product.

Business Performance Measurements. A rallying point of improvement from start to completion, intended to show whether the future state design supports the required improvements.

CIMS, Continuous Improvement Management System. A process for continuously identifying and prioritizing improvements in the process, and daily measurement of improvements over time. The closed-loop system of waste identification and elimination consisting of the following process steps: data collection by cell associates for quality, on-time delivery, productivity, and non-value added waiting time, quantified and sorted by priority by the cell. Corrective action is assigned by cell associates to a specific support team member of the appropriate skill set, who determines root cause and corrective/counter measures.

CSR, Customer Service Representative. A person who interfaces with the customers, operations, accounting, and salespeople, with the primary function of serving the customer.

Customer Cell Schedule. A schedule of product to build by required date, level loaded to meet the final assembly cell capacity and take the guesswork out of scheduling,

Customer order consolidation grid. A specific customer order consolidation point, used to eliminate the process of storing finished goods on racks. In contrast, the Lean Roadmap process assembles product to order and date, and the product is sent to an order consolidation point. At the time of order booking, a customer shipping route table is accessed, and the sales order is assigned an order consolidation grid location in shipping. As each final assembly cell completes line items for the customer order by date, the product is picked up several times/day and delivered to the consolidation point for completion.

Cellular floor plan, cell design. Cells are a logical grouping of process steps and equipment required to assemble, test, and pack a product ready for shipment to the customer. Cells are developed and designed based on product planning families. Maximum demand is forecasted for each cell, based on a Takt time calculation for the month. Internal supplier cells that supply the final assembly cells are also designed based on family forecast, Takt time, and cell constraint time.

The material flow, based on a spaghetti diagram, is used to lay out the factory with the least amount of movement. Cells are generally laid out in U or straight-line design, based on two primary factors: product size, volume, and the need to run the cell with a varying number of employees based on customer demand Takt time. Utilizing the PPQ, standardized work, 5S, Takt time, and kanban rules, cells are designed to meet customer demand, yielding significant improvement in productivity,

Cellular one piece mixed model flow. A principal requirement of lean Roadmap, is the cell design ability to assemble to customer order all variations of product within a product planning family for quantities of one for and variation. The process should be designed to produce a quantity of one for each variation of the planning family with no change over time required.

Dispatch list. Customer orders are sorted by family part #, due date, and quantity on a final assembly cell dispatch list. The CSR macro-schedules the cell, but the cell associates micro-schedule the assembly for the day/week and are free to arrange the build sequence for maximum productivity, as long as customer dates are met. Work orders are opened and closed automatically in the cell, using bar code scanning from the dispatch list or CRT/monitor screen. A routine of backflushing is used when the order is closed and the inventory to finished goods transaction is completed. Work orders are only required as a means of managing accounting requirements in the MRP/ERP logic.

Forecast, sales. An estimation of future customer requirements based on historical sales, market intelligence, new products, sales promotions, and cyclical trends. The forecast is the product quantity used by each planning family to plan the supply chain levels of product and resources required.

Furniture. The equipment to be moved into manufacturing cells.

Kanban process. A process for reorder and replenishment of point-of-use inventory. As inventory is consumed at final assembly cells and at kanban replenishment supermarket locations, the associates working in those areas reorder the material as required. If a manual card system is used, a card is sent to the supplier and used as the scheduling device based on the kanban lead-time. If electronic kanban is used, the card is scanned and a reorder message sent to the supplier. For internal suppliers, the reorder shows up on the cell dispatch list.

Kanban material flow. The kanban process is mapped based on material flow, and an internal resources person travels a predetermined route through the factory at specific times to pick up and deliver completed kanbans and customer orders, and to deliver kanban cards to supplying cells (not required if done electronically). The reorder process is managed by the point-of-use consumer and the supplier.

Lean Organization Structure. The eleven building blocks of Lean roadmap are organizationally assigned to specific people within the business. This defined group of people are then the lean organization, reporting to a senior management position responsible for the success. The defined lean organization provides a focused and defined process for each of the eleven building blocks and is then implemented throughout the business with a consistent defined process.

Manufacturing weighted average lead-time days. A calculation of lead-time based on the weighted average of the item on order: the quantity on order times the standard cost of the product, times the lead-time, divided by the total quantity on order for all products. This measurement tells us how well we are managing supply chain lead-times by weighted average standard costs and lead-times.

MRPII/ERP. Manufacturing Requirements Planning and/or Enterprise Requirements Planning. Abbreviated names for business software used for planning and accounting of manufacturing businesses.

Non-Value Added. A process step that does not add value to the product but does add cost. Typical non-value added items are inspection, queue times, rework, scrap.

PPQ, Product Process Quantity. A weighted average calculation used to determine resources required to meet a forecast of families of product. This information is used for cell design and factory layout in the future state. The process yields information required to develop a material flow in hours/days as opposed to weeks/months.,

Product Family (Product Process Planning Family). Products sold by the business with similar component structures, manufacturing steps to build, and market functions. Significant reduction in the supply chain planning process occurs as the business implements lean design based on product families. Materials, floor space, and people required are reduced.

Planning Process Family Bills of Material (MRP/ERP). This reduces planning for a family to one (1) sales planning family number per family of products.

Product family forecast. One quantity per planning family per planning period is used to forecast an entire family of products sold.

S&OP/Sales & Operations Planning. A total company business plan developed each planning cycle in minutes/hours, which provides the information required for cell capacity establishment and order scheduling ATC, kanban recalculation, supplier planning, and a rough cut financial plan. This process unites the business with a common forecasted sales plan for both sales and operations. The significant **inputs** to S&OP are the recent sales history by S&OP family, market intelligence, and cyclical impacts. The plan includes:

1. The forecast by planning family. The forecast is the input to the MRP/ERP software, and the significant **outputs** are:
2. Kanban calculations based on S&OP
3. Supplier 1 line per item planning report (issued at least weekly) for supply chain management
4. Establishment of daily/weekly capacity for final assembly cells that will assemble customer orders. (This is the order management/scheduling database called ATC, available to capacity, and is measured in units/week based on a weighted average cycle time from the forecast by unit model/part#.)

Set-Up Reduction. Set-up time is measured as the time between the moment the last good piece is completed and the time the first good piece is completed from the next product variation. Set up reduction is the application of a specific process used to reduce set up time. The set up reduction process categorizes set up into elements by class **internal, external, and unnecessary**, making identification of non-value added steps easy to identify and eliminate.

Spaghetti Diagram. As product/material makes it way from the receiving dock to finished goods and through all of the steps required to produce a product, a material flow traced on a plant layout is called a spaghetti diagram. Just as when you look at a bowl of spaghetti, not much logic is visible in the flow of material. The objective in lean is to reduce the number of flow steps.

Standardized Work. A process for identifying elements of work required to manufacture a product within a cell. As Takt time varies, a standardized work-manning chart makes it easy to divide work among varying levels of cell resources to meet the varying customer demand. Standardized work also defines how product is to be manufactured each time and without variation in the method.

Supplier 1-Line MRP Planning Report. A supply-chain planning and management report/data file that defines requirements for material for the next four weeks, and the following 2-4 monthly periods. The data is released weekly to suppliers. The first week's requirements are the kanban and non-kanban material that is to be delivered. The following weeks and months are forecasted and used for supplier planning. The Supplier 1 line per item MRP planning report is a key tool for reducing supplier lead-times.

Supply Chain. The flow of material from suppliers to manufacturing to customers, and the flow of information from customers to manufacturing to suppliers. The goals are to identify/quantify supply chain lead-time and reduce that lead-time, and speed the flow of information and material through the supply chain.

Supply Chain Planning. The output from sales and operations planning, and the adjustment of the supply chain material and resources to meet forecasted customer demand.

Supply Chain Management. The process that matches capacity to customer demand utilizing ATC, and the process of replenishing kanbans as customers consume product.

Supplier weighted average lead-times days. A valid measurement of supplier lead-time based on a weighted average value, placing greater emphasis on high-cost shipments rather than high-cost parts alone. Calculated as the weighted average of on-order quantity times standard cost, times lead-time days, divided by total quantity of product on open order at the time.

Takt Time. The drumbeat rate of demand for product being ordered by the customer—the rate that products must be produced to meet customer demand. The calculation for the Takt time = the hours available per shift/day to produce product divided by the units required per shift/day by the customers. Resources required to meet Takt time = total standard time to produce 1 unit of product/Takt time.

TPM, Total Preventative Maintenance. Performing required preventative maintenance based on quality levels, downtime, and run time intervals. Once implemented, the process reduces product variation and unplanned downtime.

Value Added. The work required to manufacture a product, bringing it to a finished state, that meets an engineering/customer specification for the product. All other steps that add cost but not value are non-value added.

Value Stream. A product process planning family, quantified by valuing all process steps required to manufacture the product.

VSM, Value Stream Map. The detailed steps required to manufacture a product process planning family product. The steps are quantified and classified according to value added and non-value added.

5S. A five-step process for establishing a workplace with a place for everything and everything in its place. This process can be used for a single station, a cell, or an entire factory.

INDEX

About The Author

First as a member of a senior management team and more recently as a business consultant specializing in lean manufacturing implementation, Howard Thomes has enjoyed a long career of business improvement and turn-around assignments, small and large. His experiences led him to write **Lean Roadmap**, a step-by-step process illustrating the building block steps that must be mapped and designed to ensure a successful lean implementation.

Lean Roadmap is a relatively new term, and the processes defined in this book will also be new to many of you. The author has successfully implemented lean processes at many manufacturing businesses and has worked with aggressive management and implementation teams as both an employee and external resource.

This book is a contribution to those of you who are struggling with lean—what to do and how to get there. **Lean Roadmap** removes the mystique of lean, and will make the lean improvement process at your business logical. A company president or CEO who lacks the time to be

191

sufficiently trained in the lean practices will easily learn the process steps required to achieve the desired results.

Howard Thomes began his "real job" career as a machinist/toolmaker and progressed to Vice President of Manufacturing Operations for a successful division of a Fortune 1000 business. In 1991, he formed Bottom Line Consultants, a virtual business model, with a pool of seasoned professionals who are called upon to support client needs as required. This business model allows for the matching of resources to specific client needs, providing real value in shortened implementation times.

Testimonials

Frank Olejack, Plant Manager
F.L. Smidth Company

"We used the Lean Roadmap concepts in a step by step process under the direction of Howard Thomes and his team in introducing Lean manufacturing techniques in our machining process. We improved our in process flow, reduced inventory and handling of the product, lowered cost and reduced our manufacturing cycle. The learning experience has been extremely valuable and we have continued to use lean concepts in all our projects. With the Lean Roadmap your organization will become smarter. The entire project has benefited us in improving our on-time deliveries and made us smarter in planning all our lean manufacturing projects."

Printed in the United States
46643LVS00003B/157